THE NEW SECONDARY EDUCATION

A Phi Delta Kappa Task Force Report

By
Maurice Gibbons

Phi Delta Kappa, Inc.
Bloomington, Indiana
1976

Library of Congress Catalog Card Number: 75-26386
ISBN 0-87367-762-3 paper
ISBN 0-87367-763-3 cloth

TABLE OF CONTENTS

Appendices

Preface

This volume is the first product of Phi Delta Kappa's Task Force on Compulsory Education and Transitions for Youth, a body suggested by the fraternity's 33rd Biennial Council in October, 1973 and authorized by the Board of Directors in January, 1974. Goals for the Task Force were outlined at a meeting held in March, 1974 at the Denver offices of the Education Commission of the States. Planners there were Martin Essex (chairman), B. Frank Brown, Howard Johnson, Maurice Gibbons, Ron Smith, and myself.

A three-phase scenario for the Task Force was drafted at that meeting. In the first phase, a leadership group would be asked to prepare a platform statement which might serve as a foundation for further work by the Task Force and, some of us dared hope, as a guide for a major reform effort in secondary education throughout America.

It is now apparent that those hopes, while optimistic, were not quixotic. The Task Force included people* who understand the problems of youth and hold strong convictions about the proper role of the high school in serving youth. After their initial discussions, they entrusted Maurice Gibbons with preparation of the platform statement, a task to which he devoted a great deal of his time during a 1975-76 sabbatical. His work was completed in the spring of 1976.

The Task Force was reorganized in May, 1976 in preparation for the second phase of its work, the organization of pilot experiments in which to test ideas presented in the platform statement. Members of the new group are Robert Binswanger, B. Frank Brown, Willard Duckett, John C. Esty, Jr., Ann E. Fitzpatrick, William Kendrick, Robert N. King, Joe Nathan, Dale Parnell, Gary Phillips, Scott Thomson, and myself. Others will be added.

This group solicits the cooperation of school districts willing and able to implement the ideas presented in this volume.

—Stanley Elam

*Members of the Task Force are listed on page vi.

MEMBERS OF THE PHI DELTA KAPPA TASK FORCE ON COMPULSORY EDUCATION AND TRANSITIONS FOR YOUTH

B. Frank Brown, director, Information and Services, Institute for Development of Educational Activities, Inc.

James S. Coleman, professor of sociology, University of Chicago

Stanley Elam, editor, *Phi Delta Kappan*

John C. Esty, Jr., staff associate, Rockefeller Family Fund

B. Keith Rose, professor of secondary education, Chico State University, deceased

Francis X. Sutman, chairman, department of secondary education, Temple University

Scott D. Thomson, associate secretary, National Association of Secondary School Principals

Maurice Gibbons, professor of education, Simon Fraser University (chairman)

This book is dedicated to colleagues and students in all the Scholars' Retreats; the Open Classroom Project; the Clinical School Collaborative; Stop the City . . . We Want to Get On!; Theme C; Experience Weeks; Walkabout; and Learning About Ourselves, Others, and the Environment. They were my teachers.

Author's Guide

An Invitation to the Reader

This proposal is as precise a blueprint for the reconstruction of education for youth as the Phi Delta Kappa Task Force on Compulsory Education and Transitions for Youth could prepare within the time allowed, and as the author could manage within the limits of his knowledge and experience. But the assignment was complex, and our accomplishment unavoidably incomplete. For this reason we invite our readers to contribute to the refinement of any of the partly formed elements of this proposal.

The arguments presented here will undoubtedly be debated and criticized in other forums; that is as it should be. What we seek are constructive ideas, evidence, practices, examples, corrections, and additions which will help us strengthen this particular approach to education for adolescents while it is still in the conceptual stage. We urge readers to approach this report from that perspective.

Submissions received by Phi Delta Kappa will be collected, analyzed, and made available in an appropriate form. The author of any material quoted or referred to will be acknowledged. To assist us in organizing responses, please use the following format:

1. Identify the element of the platform statement referred to in your contribution.
2. State the main idea of your contribution in a sentence or two.
3. Write your comment as if for publication.
4. Write your name, position, and mailing address.

The Task Force hopes this statement will be widely discussed and the elements further developed. Your responses will be part of that dialogue and will be used for that purpose.

One comment about the language used in this statement. When improvement in familiar forms of public education is described in the literature, major points of reference remain unchanged, and the meaning of such terms as "schooling," "school," "curriculum," and "learning" remain stable. But when an attempt is made to describe basic changes in the nature of public education, the meaning of such terms is inescapably affected. In the chapters which follow, some terms shift in meaning as new practices and structures are described, and some new terms are coined. "Education" is often substituted for "schooling," for instance, when the program referred to involves formal as well as informal studies conducted in settings quite different from the traditional school. Similarly, "learning" in the new program refers to the accomplishment of the personal and social transformations of adolescence as well as the mastery of academic content and school.

Acknowledgments

Colleagues and friends gave me a great deal of support and assistance in the preparation of this book. I am grateful to them. Stanley Elam, acting for the Phi Delta Kappa Board of Directors, brought together the Task Force on Compulsory Education and Transitions for Youth, arranged our meetings, and gave me the benefit of his editorial expertise and his friendship. Serving on the Task Force confirmed my esteem for members I had known through their work and generated respect for those I came to know during our sessions. Our first meeting, in October, 1974, was the most productive and compelling committee workshop I have ever attended. In such sessions, the Task Force generated the basic concepts on which this report is based, and in reviews of draft versions we refined this final statement. It would be stronger had the benefit of their counsel been available more often and for longer periods of time. Because our consultation was limited, the responsibility for excesses, inconsistencies, and other weaknesses is mine.

My colleagues on the faculty and in the graduate school classes at Simon Fraser University, and those in the public schools who debated with me the issues raised in this book, were of great help in enriching and clarifying many of the statements that appeared in early drafts of the manuscript. Colleagues across the country responded without hesitation to my requests for information and assistance: Vernon H. Smith of Indiana University; Larry McClure, Tom Owens, and other staff members at the Northwest Regional Educational Laboratory in Portland; Stanley Bippus, superintendent of Craig City School District, Alaska; Patrick Struve of the Wisconsin Center for the Study of Cognitive Learning; Howard Johnson from the University of Washington; Dirk Schenkkan of Yale Law School; Stephen Arons of the University of Massachusetts; and many others. Barbara Carter, Wayne Dobson, and Barry Kennedy, research assistants at Simon Fraser University, gathered and organized much of the basic information for me. Graeme Nelson, Ellis Paul, Rozanne Mack, Janet Yamamoto, and other members of the staff helped in many ways to get the manuscript finished and typed. I thank them all.

My family is indulgent, but will be happy, I think, to reach the end of the long silence. When I put this pencil down for the last time to go upstairs, I'll thank them in person—if anyone is still there.

Maurice Gibbons
May, 1976

CHAPTER I

Secondary Education:
The Gathering Reform

The Situation

The crucial issue of secondary education, and perhaps of all public education, is how to promote the successful transition of youth from childhood and school to adulthood and the community.

The transition from childhood to adulthood and from life in public school to life as a fully functioning member of society is, at present, a jolt. School simply ends for students. It is possible for them to graduate, even to graduate with honors, and be unprepared to choose their work, function in a job, learn a job requiring special skills, manage their personal affairs, choose a partner and establish a family, form relationships, work cooperatively in formal and informal situations, meet responsibilities as citizens in local, national, and international affairs, or continue learning on their own. Students may be unskilled in decision making and planning, the fundamental processes of adult life. They may have little or no idea of what they can do, of their capabilities for productive activities acknowledged and respected by society. And they may have few resources for, or experience with, facing obstacles, solving problems, and overcoming difficulties which can litter the path of adult life. School cannot prepare students so that they will move effortlessly into fully functioning adulthood, but the chasm can be narrowed. Bridges can be built. Unnecessary obstacles can be removed. And, equipped with experience, knowledge, and skills, young persons can be prepared for the struggle to become themselves and fully functioning adults and citizens.

For more than a dozen years after the publication of James B. Conant's book *The American High School Today* in 1959—and the renewed attention it received after the first Russian satellite was launched and Admiral Rickover's well publicized book *American Education: A National Failure* appeared in 1963—no comprehensive studies of the secondary school were made. A number of writers warned of increasing alienation of the young from institutions and society, and Theodore Roszak warned, in *The Making of a Counter-Culture*, that if schools had remained the same, adolescents and their culture certainly had not. Concern about secondary education arose again as the incidence of school disruption and violence and the rate of drug use increased alarmingly. The costs of education soared while scores on achievement tests fell. As evidence accumulated that secondary schools were not providing appropriate learning opportunities for a large portion of their constituency, it also appeared that most high schools were unable or unwilling to change to meet these pressing needs.

Finally, in 1972, the first of several important reports by national and international committees appeared. The high school, these reports declare, is in crisis. The need to offer adequate and appropriate educational opportunity to the majority of students, cultivating rather than confounding their maturity, has become a national emergency. The number of reports and the prestige of the panels and their sponsoring agencies, combined with an emerging consensus about the nature of the problems and the most promising suggestions for improvements, amount to a major educational movement for the reform of the secondary school.

The Reform Movement: Four Reports

These reports, the textbooks of the reform movement, are now essential background and guide to any work in secondary education. A number of national studies such as the National Association of Secondary School Principals' *American Youth in the Mid-Seventies* and the reports of such state-sponsored groups as California's Commission for Reform of Intermediate and Secondary Education are not reviewed here but are important additions to this growing body of work. The four summarized in the following pages combine comprehensive analysis of the problems with extensive recommendations for solving them. They are the foundations on which much of this proposal is constructed.

The Faure Report

In 1972 the International Commission on the Development of Education, established by Unesco under the leadership of Edgar Faure, released its relatively unsung but significant report, *Learning to Be: The World of Education Today and Tomorrow*. In it representatives of both Eastern and Western countries agree that education must be completely restructured to remove all barriers, requirements, and artificial distinctions impeding access to the schooling people want and need. Education, they state, should become "a true mass movement," a lifelong pattern integrating education and work with leisure, a recurrent pattern of students leaving and returning to their studies without penalty at any time. Artificial distinctions among levels (elementary, secondary, or graduate school), kinds (academic and vocational institutions), and places (in school and out of school) of education should be eliminated, making it possible for students to receive the education appropriate to them and their circumstances when they wish. Access to any form of learning at any time, and to any form of employment, should no longer be conditional upon accumulated records. Rather, it should depend upon the ability of the students assessed at the time they present themselves for it. All hierarchical distinctions among staff and faculty members, from primary teachers to university professors, should be eliminated. To provide these greatly extended opportunities for learning, educational institutions must greatly expand the range of services they offer, and such elements of the community as business and industry must share responsibility for technical and other forms of training, which they are much better equipped to provide than are the schools.

The commission argues that all programs, both primary and secondary, should have "a combined theoretical, technological, practical, and manual character." All subjects for all students should be developed with a careful balance between theoretical studies and practical work, rather than as separate programs or tracks for groups of students. If students develop a solid grounding in scientific principles and the ability to apply them technically, they will not graduate with outdated, job-specific skills but with ability to adapt to a variety of occupations. These programs should be provided in many ways, using the latest media and techniques for information processing.

The commission emphasizes that the central purpose of education is self-education. Students must learn to teach themselves, learn by teaching others, and learn by being involved in educational decisions which affect them. They must ultimately decide what they want to learn and how and where to learn it. To encourage this process, the most prepotent aids to self-help education—laboratories, data banks, mass media, video cassettes and discs—should be integrated into all learning systems.

The teachers graduated today, the commission points out, will still be teaching after the year 2000. Teachers in training, therefore, should learn the latest techniques by using the latest techniques. They should be taught not merely to transmit knowledge, but also to become specialists in organizing learning activities and in organizing learners of all ages for education in and out of school. At the same time, "skilled auxiliaries from the trades and professions" should be brought in as teachers as well as aides. This interaction between school and community should be extended to making decisions about the educational system. Above all, the commission declares, a universal basic education, geared to national needs, must be guaranteed for all children on earth suffering from "today's famine in education."

The Brown Report

In 1973 the National Commission on the Reform of Secondary Education, established by the Charles F. Kettering Foundation and led by B. Frank Brown of /I/D/E/A/, issued *The Reform of Secondary Education.* This report identified the high school as a troubled institution which was failing to accomplish its mission of equal and adequate universal education for American youth and in the larger cities was "on the verge of complete collapse." The commission said that despite a steep rise in the cost of education to the taxpayer and a decade of innovations, little, if any, improvement in the quality or effectiveness of educational programs had been made. The slowly changing school has failed to keep up with a rapidly changing society. Research has produced only a few significant findings and fewer practical recommendations. Now the boom in educational expenditure is over. There will be fewer students and less money in the future. On these grounds the commission calls for sweeping reforms pressed forward by community action and changes in public policy to provide a wide variety of alternatives in addition to much improved traditional schooling for education in both the cognitive and affective domains.

The commission makes recommendations for a broad range of specific changes:

1. Goals: Every school and the community it serves should formulate educational goals, objectives, and performance criteria and should cooperate in pursuing their achievement.

2. General Elements of Revision: Curriculum should be revised to meet these educational goals and should concentrate on students' needs and interests rather than on subjects and programs needed for college

counseling in seeking a full range of possible careers.

To insure such fair treatment, a committee for affirmative action should be established with representation from students, faculty, and the community to report to the administration on instances of inequality or discrimination.

10. Compulsory Education: The legal school attendance age should be dropped to age 14. Employment laws should be rewritten to assure students of on-the-job training. Legislation should be enacted to guarantee students fourteen years of tuition-free education so that after the compulsory eight they may seek six years of schooling where and when they wish.

By taking such explicit positions on such a range of specific issues, the commission not only outlines the range of changes which must be made in any major reform, but also sets the stage for pointed debate about them.

The Coleman Report

Youth: Transition to Adulthood, a report prepared by the Panel on Youth of the President's Science Advisory Committee (James S. Coleman, chairman), broadens and deepens the argument for the reform of education for high school age youth. It argues for education which is not limited to the development of the intellect, but is designed to cultivate other aspects of maturation necessary for successful transition to adulthood. It broadens the field also by arguing that society must reform old settings and create new ones expressly for the cultivation of this process, even if that means going beyond the plant and power of the school.

The panel strengthens the argument by providing a comprehensive history of the place of youth in our society, focusing on such changes as:

1. The world of the maturing child once dominated by the home is now monopolized formally by the school and informally by the child's age group.

2. Young persons once introduced to work as quickly as possible to aid the family are now being kept as long as possible in school, out of the labor force, to increase their potential for productivity.

3. Industrialization, universal education, and burgeoning population have led from the one-room school of eight grades to grade level isolation in large schools; from early participation in the work of the family to segregation from the adult world. To cultivate their development, the young should relate to peers of all ages in school and to adults in the community.

4. From early labor laws to restrain the exploitation of children to recent Supreme Court decisions confirming their rights, the legal status of young people has been improving. The recognition of rights to due process, freedom from arbitrary standards, and participation in decision making in school are increasing, and the constitutionality of compulsory education laws is being challenged.

5. Youth are staying at home longer and in the school system longer and are facing a rising teen-age unemployment rate even in casual work where few vocational skills are learned. As a result they are increasingly isolated, economically dependent, and deprived of maturing experiences. The full impact of this greatly increased body of well-educated but underemployed and disappointed youth has yet to be felt.

6. The age period from 14 to 24 is characterized by great diversity in the rate of physical, intellectual, and social development, by increasing differentiation of interests and abilities, by growing heterosexual interests and need for emancipation from parents, and by crises in establishing autonomy, initiative, and identity.

7. The fact that adolescents are generally more rapid and efficient learners than younger children suggests delaying some or all training until the age of maximum efficiency. In the panel's analysis, those

attending school only half time performed as well as
full-time students on achievement tests.

8. As the population of 13- to 17-year-olds in school
   grew in the 1930s, adolescents became a distinctive
   social group which by the 1950s had developed its
   own cultural norms. By the 1970s large numbers of
   this group were staying together still longer. A new
   period of life termed "youth" emerged, and with it a
   youth culture distinguished by unique patterns of
   activity (dress, music) and diverse subgroups (drug,
   athletic, political, religious, and mystical) but characterized by the young looking to the young for interaction, support, and behavioral norms, by increasing regard for youth who successfully challenge
   adults, by concern for the underdog, and by an interest in change. These features are attributed to the
   large number of youth, their affluence (with parental
   money), their access to a wide range of communications media, and their segregation from adults and
   adult institutions.

In an effort to steer education in the direction of experiences, training, and productive activity which focus on
major aspects of maturation, the panel makes the following recommendations:

1. Changes in School Structure: The trend toward comprehensive schools should be reversed to permit
   schools to be smaller (no larger than 500 students)
   and specialized in teaching emphasis (e.g. performing arts, science, humanities, and sectors of business
   and industry), offering students a choice in schooling. In addition, the school should become an agency
   for the young, delegating a portion of its custody
   and time to other institutions in the community
   which it organizes and makes available to students.
   A greater range of experiences should be offered
   within the school as well by raising the status of
   certain extracurricular and less academic subjects
   and by involving students in tutoring younger pupils.

2. Alternation of School and Work: The panel proposes

experimentation with two patterns: First, with a tri-semester system in which one semester of work is balanced against two semesters of school for college-bound as well as vocational students; and second, with the more familiar half-time work, half-time study alternation.

3. Work Organizations: Business and industry should receive financial support for creating roles and providing training for youth.

4. Youth Communities and Organizations: The panel proposes the establishment of largely self-governing nonresidential youth communities designed to combine studies with providing public service or producing marketable goods. Further, it proposes government support for such adult-sponsored youth organizations as the Y.M.C.A. and the Boy Scouts if they will extend their activities in the public service field. In addition, they urge the government to experiment with greatly expanded public service projects such as the Peace Corps but located in America and designed exclusively for youth 16 to 24 years old.

5. Legislation to Facilitate Youth Employment: The panel recommends that constraints which severely limit job opportunities for youth be reexamined and modified within the demands of protection: child labor standards, minimum wage levels, employer administrative procedures, and other barriers which discourage employers from hiring youth.

6. Vouchers: To give students the choice of where they will be educated and when, and to make educational institutions more responsive to the nature and interests of youth, the panel recommends experimentation with giving students vouchers, at age 16, bearing the value of four years of college education.

The panel's recommendations intended to implement these concepts: education should cultivate maturation; experiences should be designed to accomplish this growth; society should participate in determining these choices; and the school should be only one of several possible agencies and settings in which the educational process can occur.

The Martin Report

In 1974 the National Panel on High Schools and Adolescent Education, appointed by the U.S. Office of Education largely from the ranks of scholars and led by John Henry Martin, circulated a discussion draft of its findings. It provides a status report on secondary education in the United States, identifies and analyzes current problems of adolescent education, recommends reforms, describes the policy issues involved, and outlines needed research. In this tentative draft stage of the report, the panel confirms the school as the basic institution of education. It concurs with the other reports, criticizing the large comprehensive high school, isolation of adolescents from younger children and adults, the school's failure to recognize earlier maturation of the young, inadequacies in curriculum and organizational structure, the secondary school's inability to change with the demands of the times, and their willingness to become, in the panel's most famous phrase, "aging vats" for the young.

The panel said, "The conclusion is inescapable that the comprehensive high school has failed to fulfill its promise." It has failed to provide true breadth of courses to the mass of students. It emphasizes and perpetuates class and racial differences. It creates a three-track culture—academic, general, and vocational—in which only the academic track is given sufficient attention. Fully 50 percent of high school students are in the general track, which prepares them for neither work nor college. Large comprehensive high schools tend to be inhumane, bureaucratic, and unsuited to meeting individual needs; they tend to foster alienation of students from their peers and their environment; and they tend to have more problems with attendance, disruption, and violence. In summary, "The evidence about the psychological effect of a large school is impressively, consistently negative." In response to this situation,

> The panel feels that the solution lies in . . . structural and conceptual change . . . which gets away from the notion that education can only go on in a classroom with disciplined students listening obediently to one teacher for a specific block of time.

The major directions of structural and conceptual change the panel considers are toward

1. Educating adolescents to become full and responsible members of society.
2. Creating a climate and program which respects individual differences.
3. Preparing adolescents for future familial roles and for work.
4. Integrating institutions of education and the broader community.
5. Preparing adolescents to participate knowledgeably in the decision-making process of society.
6. Providing aesthetic experiences for adolescents and guidance in coping with the media.

To move in these directions, the panel recommends shifting the emphasis from creating catch-all comprehensive schools to providing a comprehensive education appropriate for youth. In curriculum, this means a balance of experience and studies in five domains: 1) *Personal Values*—studying issues of individual identity, independence, and social interaction. 2) *Citizenship*—developing personal values and their relationship to community goals through active participation in the political realm intended to inspire caring, cooperativeness, and a "lively concern for the common good" among students. 3) *The Arts*—developing an aesthetic sense through participation in artistic activity and guided experience in excellent artistry. 4) *The Humanities*—learning the disciplines of inquiry through which a person examines the objectifiable aspects of the human condition in order to understand and to act wisely. 5) *Technics*—studying applied knowledge, the technologies and processes of production and service which use the results of detached inquiry to improve the quality of life in a morally responsible way, and the jobs and careers which employ them.

How can learning in these domains best be accomplished? Although it has "not achieved any great and cogent illuminations about the reordering of education," the panel recommends many program and organizational changes worth examining in detail. They include:

1. Extending education into the community for voluntary participation in social and governmental service agencies, for "real jobs with real work for youth," for experience and training in specialized community centers for activities such as the performing arts, and for participation in social, political, and governmental community activities so that the most suitable contexts for desired learning can be chosen.

2. Making secondary schools more diverse, smaller, and more inclusive of a variety of learning sites; by bringing artists and other adults into the school to teach; by making conduct, relationships, and decision making within the school a model of democratic participation; by making the regular day from two to four hours long, and making those hours more powerful; and by reconsidering compulsory education laws.

3. Restructuring the organization of schools to include governance by broad participation in decisions about the school's function, the establishment of coordinating agencies to facilitate and monitor students' out-of-school experiences, and the exploration of "process models" of administration through interaction rather than through hierarchical staff organization.

The panel is convinced that schools do make a difference, that they are essential to democracy, and that they should remain the institution of formal learning, but they must come under rigorous examination and be systematically improved.

Enter, the *Kappan*

While these reports began appearing, the *Phi Delta*

Kappan and several other publications were zeroing in on
one major question in the reform debate: Is the legal requirement for children to receive public education until
they are 16 years of age a major factor in the unrespon-
siveness of secondary schools? Compulsory school attendance seems to be the foundation of the present system, a
guarantee of both its student constituency and its practices.
From the student point of view, it guarantees that one
must take it, leave it, or buy an expensive private education. A number of adversaries claim that the only way to
open up alternatives to familiar schooling is to lower the
age of compulsory education and offer students a choice
of alternative routes to work and high school graduation.
To explore this issue in detail, Phi Delta Kappa established the Task Force on Compulsory Education and Transitions for Youth.

The Task Force was charged with determining whether
it would be advantageous to lower the age of compulsory
education, and if it would, to determine for what reasons
and by what means it should be done and what alternatives
should be made available to students. At the initial meeting of the Task Force, however, discussion made it clear
that the issue of compulsory education was only one part
of a larger complex of issues. The basic need was identified as the development of educational services to cultivate the transition of youth to adulthood and functioning
membership in society. The results of a survey made at Phi
Delta Kappa district conferences in 1974 showed that the
membership shared the concerns of the Task Force. Of
the eighteen propositions examined at these conferences,
two of the issues identified as most crucial were:

> How can the schools promote both the development of
> individual initiative and independence on one hand and
> social responsibility on the other?

> How can educational systems adapt to the demand for al-
> ternative routes to adulthood for students not well served
> by the traditional secondary school program?

By this time the four reports on the reform of secondary

education were available. With this extensive groundwork already accomplished, the Task Force decided not to repeat such investigations but to consolidate the arguments and prepare a guide for developing a model of schooling designed to promote the transition of youth.

The process involves three stages, with progress from one stage to the next contingent upon approval by Phi Delta Kappa:

1. Prepare a platform statement recommending a form of secondary education for the transition of youth and a means of establishing it.
2. Conduct a pilot project or projects in which the model and the process are field-tested and refined through three years of developmental modification.
3. Report on the pilot project, its nature, the history of modifications in the project, the results, and recommendations arising from the three-year study.

This report completes the first stage of the five-year process.

The Task Force Report

Chapter 2 explores the problems which the Task Force was formed to examine: If students are not required by law to attend school until they are 16, will those who leave early benefit? Will secondary schools be stimulated to provide more appropriate programs for those who choose to remain? Attempting to change the schools simply by changing the law does not seem a promising course, but some of the changes widely recommended—sending students out of school and placing them in jobs, for instance—seem possible only when attendance, and therefore participation, is voluntary. However, the consequences and benefits of reducing the age of compulsory education are little known.

But what kind of programs are most appropriate? Chapter 3 identifies fourteen propositions on which the reformation of secondary education might be based. The emphasis is on ways of increasing the impact of schooling on learning: intensifying the use of teaching time, gearing school to human development, including intense experience and practical productive activities as well as theoretical studies in all learning sequences, involving students in activities with adults in the community, mobilizing the available social forces for learning, and improving school programs with a process of continual and systematic development.

Many forms of schooling could be developed from these propositions. The Task Force, in search of a model promising enough to implement in a pilot study, discovered the Carleton School District, which has developed a system of secondary education employing many practices implicit in the propositions. The Carleton operation is described in Chapter 4 to illustrate the practices described more theoretically in the presentation of the model developed by the Task Force in Chapter 5. Both the practical applications of Carleton and the theory of the Task Force emphasize intense but differentiated schools at the junior stage during which students spend two months at each of eight different sites, each having a unique teaching focus. At the next step, secondary levels, students work individually and in groups primarily on challenges in the areas of adventure, inquiry, aesthetics, practical applications, academics, service, and work. Students, however, may pursue options to these central programs in a number of ways. The community is widely used and deeply involved in the school system. Particularly important is the involvement of community adults as well as educators on the advisory council, which manages the programs.

This theoretical model of a system for cultivating the maturity of youth cannot be fully established in local educational systems as they presently exist. If it is ever to be successfully implemented, a new and appropriate setting must be created in school districts—one in which the environment, conditions, materials, and personnel are carefully prepared to support rather than complicate the program's development. Recommendations for creating such a setting are described in Chapter 6.

The problems and inadequacies of high schooling have

been exhaustively catalogued. Lists of recommendations for solving the problems and for improving the effectiveness of high school programs have been compiled. The intent of this monograph is not to extend those lists of problems and recommendations nor to seek improvements in secondary schooling as it presently exists. Recommendations without a procedure for implementation are seldom followed; improvements in a part of the system, once adopted, are usually absorbed with little or no effect. Rather, the intent here is to distill from these previous analyses and suggestions some guidelines for a new, improved form of secondary education to create a new model with its own purpose, a process designed to achieve that purpose, and a setting to support the process. Rather than attempt to improve teaching methods or some other aspect of schooling, the intent here is to formulate a comprehensive system with a powerful and beneficial influence on the learning of youth.

This means describing a model of secondary education which does not yet exist—a model with promise, perhaps, but not certainty. Even though guidelines have emerged from research and practice, formulating such a new model is inescapably speculative. Development requires going beyond the familiar and the known, however tactical the procedure. This proposal is presented with the knowledge that refinements will be necessary before the conceptualizing stage is complete, and further refinements will be required during trial operations of the system. We hope that colleagues and members of the community will assume that major development is necessary to solve the problems of secondary education, that they will consider this model in its entirety as one approach to solving those problems, and that they will join the discussion about the refinement of the proposed practices so that a promising form of education can be designed to promote the transition of our youth from childhood and school to adulthood and the community.

CHAPTER II

To Compel or
Not to Compel

Compulsory attendance and other aspects of compulsory education have become major issues in the reform of secondary education on the ground that their enforcement by the state not only abridges the rights of parents but also restrains adolescents from legitimate alternatives to school and weakens the thrust of change in secondary schools themselves. In an attempt to resolve some of these arguments, the laws and procedures governing legal educational requirements will be examined, the issues arising from these circumstances will be discussed, and finally, recommendations for the resolution of the issues will be made.

Compulsory Education in Outline

Attendance regulations, like most aspects of education in America, are determined by the individual states. Although thirty-two require students to attend school between the ages of 7 and 16, the lower and upper ages vary. In eleven states the required age of school entry is 6, and in five states the age is 8. In five states compulsory attendance terminates at age 15, in six states at 17, and in five others at 18. Mississippi dropped its attendance regulations in 1967. Although students are compelled to attend—more accurately, parents are compelled to see that their children attend—from the ages of 6 to 8 until 15 to 18, students can be exempted in several ways, usually at the discretion of the district board or superintendent.

Nearly all states will exempt the mentally retarded, chronically ill, and physically handicapped, and students receiving an alternative equivalent education in an independent school or from a private tutor. In addition, however, twenty-five states exempt students who are legally employed, fourteen of them as early as age 14. Twelve of these states and two others exempt students upon completion of a certain grade—two upon completion of grade 6, ten upon completion of grade 8—usually because legal employment requires it. In three states an academic equivalency test allows students to earn exemption by achieving a certain score; in fourteen states the district board or other local authority has discretionary powers to grant exemptions for reasons not covered in the state regulations; in five states a parent's objection can lead to exemption; and in twenty-five states a child may be exempt from compulsory school attendance under other conditions. Some states have as many as a dozen such conditions.

The responsibility for enforcing these attendance laws lies, in most cases, with the district board. State regulations usually require the board to appoint an attendance officer to maintain records of student absence and to investigate those without legal excuse. Most states require the officer to determine the cause of absence; if the officer finds it is unjustified, the parents must be ordered to comply with the law; if this fails, the child is taken into custody and the state's attorney is advised. Upon conviction, parents may be fined as much as $200 (in two states) and/or receive a jail term for one to ninety days, depending on the state and previous convictions. The regularity and intensity with which these laws are applied likely varies widely.*

Compulsory attendance, however, is only one aspect of compulsory education. Students compelled to attend school may be said to receive a compulsory education in the third degree. But if they are compelled in any way to attend a state school rather than a school of their own choice, that is compulsory education in the second degree. And if they are compelled to attend a state school in which the program is prescribed by the state,** it is first-degree compulsory education. Attending school eliminates alternatives to schooling; attending a state school because independent schools are too expensive eliminates alternative forms of schooling; attending state schools with the same prescribed program not only eliminates choice within the state system, but also challenges the rights of the individual and the family when those prescriptions go beyond basic literary skills to require the teaching of certain ideas, beliefs, and value-laden practices.

When attendance, school, and program are prescribed and enforced by state law, several issues concerning the rights of citizens are raised: the right of adults and children to freedom from unnecessary state control, the right of all to education of equal quality, and the right to certain minimum guaranteed outcomes from the years of required schooling. Such individual rights are defined by court decision in cases which test the power and responsibility of state and district authorities and the constitutionality and interpretation of the laws that grant them.

In summary, compulsory education is far more than a simple matter of school attendance. It is set down in fifty different sets of legislation and systems of practice in fifty states which allow different exemptions from schooling,

*This information is summarized from A Study of State Legal Standards for the Provision of Public Education by the Lawyer's Committee for Civil Rights Under the Law, Linda E. Perls, Project Director.

**The study by the Lawyer's Committee shows a major split in program policy: In twenty-five states the curriculum is prescribed by a state executive agency, in three by an independent state committee, and in twenty-two by local authorities working within state guidelines.

different alternatives in schools, and different degrees of prescription in the school program. Nor is compulsory education a static concept. Rather, it is a focal point of interaction between the state and the people during the passage of laws in the legislature, their interpretation by the courts, and their enactment into local school practice. The record of these interactions is a history of the people's and the state's educational concerns. Any attempt to change compulsory education must be conducted in light of these educational, legal, and historical complexities.

The Issues

The concept that all citizens should receive a basic education and that this is rightfully provided in a school system organized by the people's representatives is generally accepted.

> In almost all of the struggles over the content, structure, and methods of public schools, the underlying agreement among the combatants has been that majoritarian political control of the school system is appropriate. Whether the struggle over values takes place in a school board election, an administrator's office, or the state legislature, Americans have acknowledged, for the most part, that to have this struggle is proper and to accept its results required.*

In that important struggle, one major educational issue is whether required school attendance until the age of 16 or more serves the best interests of students. Witness these statements by recent national and international commissions and committees. From the National Commission on the Reform of Secondary Education:

> If the high school is not to be a custodial institution, the state must not force adolescents to attend. Earlier maturity—physical, sexual, and intellectual—requires an option of earlier departure from the restraints of formal schooling. The formal school leaving age should be dropped to age 14.

*Stephen Arons. "The Separation of School and State: Pierce Reconsidered." Unpublished draft, January, 1976, p. 2.

From the National Panel of High Schools and Adolescent Education:

> The Panel raises the question of the utility of the last year or two of high school if, in fact, terminal points of development have already been reached by age 15. . . . While the Panel by no means recommends the immediate elimination of compulsory education laws, we do suggest this reconsideration. . . .

From the Panel on Youth of the President's Science Advisory Committee:

> Is a fixed minimum age criterion for terminating school and beginning work appropriate? It is certainly not feasible to examine in every instance the school environment and a potential work environment and then decide the case on its merits. But it seems likely that a better means can be formed for assuring the rights of the young person to some degree of self-determination while protecting him from exploitation by others.

From the International Commission on the Development of Education:

> *Artificial or outmoded barriers between different educational disciplines, courses, and levels, and between formal and nonformal education should be abolished; recurrent education should be gradually introduced and made available.* . . . This presupposes that more students will be able to move more freely from one level to the next throughout the establishment and from one establishment to another. Students will be able to enter freely at various stages and leave at many different points.

Many basic educational arguments for reducing the age of required attendance to 14 or 15 in all states are implicit in those statements. Critics claim that students, in cooperation with parents, should be able to choose whether to remain in school and what program they will pursue both as a basic right and a necessary responsibility in preparation for adulthood. Since students are now maturing 2½ years earlier than when the laws were passed, it is argued, the laws should be changed to permit the exercise of these choices earlier.

Many educators also state that adolescents need access to work and other out-of-school experiences to cultivate their maturity but that attendance requirements obviate such opportunities. In general, innovators consider these requirements as a major cause, also, of what they perceive as the inability or unwillingness of school authorities and personnel to change their traditional practices to meet current and future possible circumstances. Because students are required to attend school, its clientele is guaranteed, leaving it with little competition and few critical standards of performance to meet and few of the normal institutional pressures to change. If the law is a major cause of school inertia, advocates of secondary school reform argue, changing the law cannot only permit, but also stimulate, the pursuit of radical improvements—particularly if the choices open to students include desirable nonschool options and alternative schools which attract large numbers of them. The law which is seen by the innovator to impede, however, is seen by many practitioners merely to require, to describe in statutes the demands of the state—confirmed by the acceptance of the people—for the form of education they provide. From an educational perspective, the issues arise in the confrontation of these two positions.

When these issues rely for their resolution on the law, a broader range of considerations is invoked. From a legal perspective, the task is not to defend or resist educational change, but to maintain a just balance between the powers of the state and the rights of the child and the parent. Although neither the Constitution nor the Bill of Rights makes any specific reference to educational rights or responsibilities, the power of the state to determine educational requirements for its residents was granted by the Tenth Amendment to the Constitution as interpreted by the Supreme Court. That power is expressed in the constitution, statutes, and regulations of each state. The Fourteenth Amendment, however, protects individual rights granted under the Constitution from any abridgment by the states, and the Tenth Amendment reserves for the people those powers not delegated to the United States or permitted to the states. This sets the stage for the basic legal confrontation on educational matters in which individuals test whether the state meets its obligations to them and whether its requirements abrogate their rights, and in which the state tests its legal authority to insure that individuals conform to its requirements. Other factors also enter this equation of authority and rights which the courts must balance in their decisions. Compulsory attendance laws, for instance, are inseparable from federal and state child labor laws which grant certain status and rights to children for their protection from abuse and which now may complicate their opportunities to find the work reformers claim they need. However, if education critics point the way in major educational changes, those dependent upon modifications in the interpretation of the law are settled in the courts, just as changes in the law itself are settled in the legislatures of each state by the people's representatives.

But are changes in the law or its interpretation sufficient to guarantee that schools will make desired changes? Changing attendance laws may be necessary to alter the conditions of schooling but seems inadequate to modify student experiences. Lowering the age of required attendance will not change other compulsory aspects of education—prescribed curricula, required subjects, assigned textbooks, and the like. To create such an effect, large numbers of students might have to leave, placing pressure on the school to develop programs attracting its clientele to return. Large numbers of students now attending might not leave as long as the social pressure to remain is great and the number of attractive out-of-school alternatives is small.

No matter what the legal conditions, changes in schooling depend upon local decisions to exercise the choices available. State requirements describe an area within which, almost without exception, degrees of freedom can be exercised by participants. Within any set of state regulations, schools can be greatly different, depending upon the degree to which teachers, parents, students, and administrators are prepared to test the limits constraining them and on the willingness of local authorities to respond to their efforts. If the schools of a particular district are characterized by constraint, passivity, and uniformity, changing the attendance laws is probably insufficient to stimulate improvements. Wide-ranging debate, a developing consensus, and change in the law or its interpretation may help alter conditions of schooling. To these must be added a strategy encouraging participants to use legitimate available means to maintain a firm engagement with local authorities, so that negotiation rather than prescription determines school practice. These means include the electoral process, lobbying, petition, the press of public opinion, the various tactics of confrontation, and court action.

The first compulsory attendance regulation was passed in 1852, and by 1917 regulations existed and were enforced in most states. Although the extent of societal support and enforcement has varied markedly from state to state and community to community, public support generally remains high. A recent Gallup Poll shows that 90 percent of the public favor compulsory elementary education and 73 percent favor compulsory attendance through the senior high school years. Only 56 percent of professional educators now favor compulsory secondary schooling and this may foreshadow a major shift in the national attitude. But any agency now attempting to lower the age from 16 to 14 will have to consider and deal with opposition from majority opinion and a strong tradition of required schooling.

One aspect of this opposition is a humanitarian desire to protect the young from a harsh world. Part of a crusade against exploitation of the young, the first compulsory education laws were passed with related legislation limiting the use of child labor. A second factor was labor's opposition to the displacement of adults in the job market by children working for lower wages. The need and desire among adults to be free from the responsibility of caring for and educating their children and to be free to seek employment was a third force. In addition, parents believed that education through the teen years gave their children a financial advantage by certifying them for better jobs. To the advantage of certification we can add the economic advantage of gaining passage to college and university, the prestige of academic programs, and the social status achieved through graduation. Reverse effects came into play when high school graduation became the norm, making nonattendance deviant behavior.*

Other factors contributing to the maintenance of compulsory education requirements include the state's obligation to provide an equal opportunity for education, first to people from every socioeconomic stratum, and more recently to people of every race, so that all citizens have an equal chance for the benefits of the society through schooling. Maintaining this equality has involved busing children of minority groups to majority schools, and now pressure is mounting for a scheme of equal financing to insure that well supported schools do not exist only in wealthy communities. If minority groups sense that lowering the age of compulsory education prejudices their children's opportunities by weakening the state's obligations, their opposition may be swift. While the state is obliged in these ways, it has the constitutional right to demand that citizens receive what education is necessary to teach them the nature and value of the democratic process and the skills necessary to participate in it. Clarifying how much education that means and the justifiable compulsion to assure it is another legal problem.

But one of the most potent forces maintaining compulsory education requirements may be the same economic pressures that led to the early regional enactments, which effectively squelched competition to the state's own schools. E. G. West, analyzing the political economy of American public school legislation, concludes that alternative choices in education ended when the rate bills parents

*This paragraph draws heavily from James B. Coleman's analysis in *Youth: Transition to Adulthood.*

paid for public schooling were eliminated by the introduction of a state tax for education in 1851. The public school lobby, he says, wiped out the threat of private schools that could no longer compete financially. Subsequently, they went into an "absolute decline." While most of the arguments in the debate focused on the welfare of the young, the acts themselves, according to West, seem to serve the self-interests of school personnel and the state's own institutions by guaranteeing a clientele and stable income. With the beginning of compulsory attendance regulations the next year and later of child labor laws, schooling was virtually locked up by the state. The benefits of universal if not universally equal education and the protection of children were assured, but at a considerable price in freedom of choice. Education, for most families, was well on the way to becoming compulsory in the first degree.

As recent American history demonstrates, the tendency of any government agency—perhaps of any institution—is to extend its power, its constituency, and its activities until some outside force checks it. Institutions cannot be expected to show thoughtful restraint or to willingly share previously consolidated authority. Educational institutions are no exception. The present situation, in which the state compels all citizens to use services it alone provides, is unique because no independent agency has adequate authority and resources to counterbalance the state's extensive control. Thus, the critical debate, the testing of rights through the courts and sustained community action are of unusual importance.

Changing the Law

While compulsory education requirements are maintained by social, educational, and legal pressures, counterpressures are accumulating. For instance, evidence presented in the four reports quoted suggests that secondary schooling is not able to deliver on all the hopes the public has placed in it; that changes in students and in society are making familiar forms of education less and less appropriate for more and more people, and that schools generally seem unable or unwilling to provide experiences necessary to prepare adolescents for adulthood. They suggest compulsory attendance regulations in practice are becoming a mockery. If students are maturing earlier, critics argue, the law should permit them to leave school earlier. If school cannot or will not provide the kind and quality of educational experience adolescents require, the law should free them to seek other options. If a law of compulsion enables the school to resist systematic educational advances by guaranteeing a clientele, lowering the legal leaving age may compel school authorities to compete in developing programs to attract students. If failure to pursue attendance-law violation is teaching students disrespect for the law, it should be changed to conform with practice so that its dignity is maintained.

But the law is changed by legal arguments, not educational ones. The legal issues are much more intricate, precise, and procedural.

One of the basic arguments against compulsory education laws is that the state, in fulfilling its legal obligation, abridges the rights of individuals. As Howard Johnson says, "I can think of no other place in our society where we attempt to make a basic right a requirement."

Carl Bereiter observes that though governments everywhere assume the right to intervene in education, it is unusual that such a "terrible affront to individual liberty" is imposed in much the same way in America as in countries where the individual is subordinated to the state. It is as if the state accepted the duty to provide elections, compelled people to exercise their right to vote, and offered one candidate, the state's. Providing education may be called a state duty; in practice it resembles a monopoly.

In examining the nature of the state's imposition, Bereiter points out that the law requires school attendance, but that a U.S. Supreme Court decision guarantees parents the right to reject public schooling and seek instruction for their children elsewhere. This choice is open only to parents with access to private schools and the money to pay for it in addition to the public schooling they refuse. Once the student is in school, how much schooling does the state require, and how compulsory is it? Bereiter cites other Supreme Court decisions which interpret the legal requirement to be basic education, the three Rs. There is less evidence that the state has a right to intervene in forming character and beliefs or to insist upon pursuing particular fields of study. Schools cannot compel students to salute the flag, and any form of religious education must be avoided, because such impositions invade "the sphere of intellect and spirit which it is the purpose of the First Amendment to our Constitution to reserve from all official control." Bereiter says he thinks that eventually parents acting on conscience will be able to reject any specific program beyond the basics. A legal precedent states, "No pupil attending the school can be compelled to study any prescribed branch against the protest of the parent."

In the meantime, the states do require attendance, and in more than half, what students will learn is emphatically delineated. Only five states provide exemption for parental objection, and then only with approval of the board or superintendent. Legal precedent suggests that students are excused only on objections in the most sensitive areas of human conduct. If these rulings protect an individual's personal beliefs from state intrusion, they do not promise to exempt a significant number of students from compulsory education generally.

Interestingly, U.S. Supreme Court decisions define the right to equal educational opportunity—but on the basis of opportunity to education as it generally exists in America, not against any definition of what the people's basic rights to education are. The Lawyers' Committee for Civil Rights Under Law points out that rights to education are more clearly established by the New Jersey Supreme Court decision in *Robinson* v. *Cahill,* in which the state and its policy makers are made responsible for defining "a thorough and efficient" education and for implementing a finance system to assure each child the opportunity for that kind of education. While such a decision contributes to equality of opportunity and to the quality of that opportunity, however, it also emphasizes the state's authority over programs as well as services.

Even a preliminary investigation of the legal aspect of compulsory education reveals that the law is a tangled web of federal and state constitutions, statutes, articles, amendments, regulations, exemptions, precedents, and procedures which trap and immobilize the public. Yet the law is clearly a powerful instrument of educational reform. To utilize this instrument, some bridge between a league of specialists in educational law and various groups seeking the improvement of education must be built, not only so that those seeking change can be informed and assisted, but also so they can learn to think of educational change in terms of legal action. Changing the compulsory attendance regulations might not have the effects educational reformers seek, or it might not be the best way, through the law, to seek the changes they desire, or among possible tactics it might not hold the greatest chance of success in a trial or vote. Changing the law in each state is an exhausting prospect. Establishing the right of parents to choose nonstate high schools without financial penalty may achieve more of the reformers' program goals, and lobbying in state capitols may be a more effective tactic than court action. Such leagues of specialists, working with independently sponsored national commissions, could more adequately counterbalance state authority in education and thereby maintain a systematic process of negotiated change. Certainly, the compulsory education issue requires further clarification by specialists in law governing education and guidance from them in how best to change the situation the law creates.

The State and the Community

What relationship should exist between the people and the state concerning the education of their children?

Institutions tend to absorb more responsibilities and to extend their authority as circumstances require or allow. Seldom do they willingly give up old functions like maintaining compulsory education, even when they are no longer necessary or desirable. When families needed the work or income of children for economic survival, and when industry employed them for cheap labor without benefit of an advocate, compulsory education protected the young from misuse and gave them the opportunity to learn skills necessary not only for functioning in a democratic society but also for their own betterment. What is necessary for the education of each child, as defined by legislative enactment, has expanded until required schooling now dominates the lives of children as thoroughly as labor once did. But times have changed. The great majority of parents want and demand education for their children. The national conversion to business and industry is over. The needs of society and the opportunities required by youth are both more complex and more diversified than a single-minded institution seems able to provide. Indeed, as several articles in a recent issue of *Saturday Review* point out, demand is rapidly growing among citizens of all ages for increasingly diverse educational opportunities.

If we are already experiencing the early stages of a movement in which individuals eagerly pursue education recurrently throughout their lives, then it may be inappropriate for the state to address the public, even through its laws, in an adversary relationship. A system designed to compel attendance is not necessarily suitable for those who choose to attend, nor is a system designed to enforce learning suitable for cooperation in learning or preparing the young for such a role. To acknowledge a present and prepare for a future in which the people rather than the state have the major initiative for education requires transforming community-school relationships. They must become characterized less by compelled rights and obligatory programs and more by the responsiveness of the system in creating services for its clients, the children and adults of the community.

Education is a service now, but interaction between the service and client is not negotiation or cooperation between two parties of equal or near-equal strength. A consultative relationship seems more probable when the relation is based less on the police model of enforcing state prescriptions and more on the medical model of a responsive and responsible service to clients.

In medical practice, for instance, the client has the right to service, the opportunity to select, the guarantee that the service chosen will be responsibly provided, and the right to withdraw or change if the service is not beneficial. In education, the student is obliged to attend school, usually has no opportunity to select from different kinds of schools, has no guarantee that the service selected will be responsibly provided, and is unable to withdraw or change without prejudice. Parents are equally limited in choices and assurances.

In a consultative relationship, rights and responsibilities are shared; client and expert interact both to determine the service required and to pursue the course of action. Of course, responsibilities go with these rights. In education the consultant would seem responsible for the quality of the professional guidance given, but responsibility for achievement would fall directly upon the client, the student, and the parents. In establishing such a relationship, the concept of rights extends from a passive guarantee against the abridgment of freedoms to an active guarantee of services that wither or flourish according to the demand their quality and appropriateness elicit from clients.

Beyond the rather modest requirements set down by the federal government, the school serves the community. It is a service to citizens, supported by citizens. It is theirs as surely as the library and the community center and the roads are theirs.

In such circumstances, it seems anomalous that arbitrary state legislation and local rulings on that legislation can dictate exactly what education children will receive without consulting with them, their parents, and other members of the community. Many districts, schools, and teachers are, of course, responsive—through community schools, for instance. But they respond within the rules or in spite of them and through goodwill rather than any duly constituted rights and procedures which assure citizens of such responsiveness. If not legally correct, it seems reasonable to suggest that citizens can rightfully demand a consultative relationship with the schools they support and which intimately affect the thinking and behavior of their children. Developing such a relationship seems consistent with emerging educational trends and necessary for cultivating a learning community in which people seek more, though different, kinds of education. It also seems a promising stimulant for an apparently moribund system needing new purpose and direction for its considerable resources and energies. In a learning society people seek education. When education is a consultative service, education not only adapts to this process but also cultivates it and becomes a necessary part of the process itself.

The transition between two radically different systems is always difficult. We may already be experiencing the first effects of the transition between compulsory educational programs and compulsory educational services. Essential to that transition will be preparing students to be more self-directing and responsible clients. The preparation devised will depend upon a new interpretation of student rights, one giving greater freedom so that they can experience the greater responsibilities accompanying autonomy. The balance of authority among children, parents, and the state must shift significantly—first, in favor of parents in relationship to the state, and second, in favor of students in relationship to both state and parents.

One expression of this shift would be a redefinition of compulsory education based on the age at which students become full-fledged clients of the community's educational service. To prepare students for the client-service relationship, the state could require schools to provide skill training and experience in self-directed learning, decision making, and action. These seem at least as important to students preparing for adulthood in a democratic society as training in basic literacy skills. Attendance could be compulsory on a graduated scale in which directed educational activity decreased while supervised but self-directed activity increased. As students matured and their skills increased, so would the time available and the range of community educational resources at their disposal, so in the graduating year they could negotiate their programs as full-fledged clients. In this way student roles and adult roles would gradually merge. As students are treated less like educational wards of the state, parents could assume more of the rights and responsibilities for supervision and students could shoulder more rights and responsibilities for learning. Bereiter points out that no legislation or precedents exist for even canvassing children's views when their desires are in conflict with their parents'. Therefore, no basis exists for establishing student rights to experience the independence required in the transition to adult autonomy. This situation could be corrected by a law granting student rights designated for the decisions in education only or by a required process of consultation involving students, their parents, and the school.

Can this client-consultant system of education work? We will only know by trial, educational and legal. The more important question is whether the goal is desirable enough to make overcoming the inevitable difficulties worth the effort.

Will Changing Attendance Laws Change Attendance?

Granting adolescents the right to leave school at an earlier age as an isolated act is an empty gesture. Though once necessary, compulsory attendance laws probably no longer retain students who want to leave in school. The laws may not be enforceable in any case. In *The Reform of Secondary Education* B. Frank Brown said,

> In 1972 the Supreme Court struck down that part of the Wisconsin law which compelled children of members of the Amish religion to attend school beyond eighth grade. . . . If Amish children cannot be compelled to go to school, it is hard to see how others can be under a rule of law that promises equal treatment to all.

Although the actual decision carefully guards against such a broad application, actual practice may be anticipating what later decisions will confirm. As Howard M. Johnson pointed out in 1974, rising absentee rates and increased student rights before the law make the cost of attendance enforcement too high for the poor results achieved. Apparently fewer schools are trying. Some have argued that the number of absentees and school-age students not enrolled who are neither pursued nor prosecuted only breeds disrespect for laws so ineffective and freely broken. For this reason alone, they should be changed.

In any case, the law is probably not keeping many students in school. The fact so many remain   after their sixteenth year suggests that large numbers of students will not respond by leaving when the required age is lowered. If it were changed tomorrow, it seems entirely possible the event would pass unnoticed. Although some find school boring, many do not. Part of the attraction is the social experience, the peer culture, which draws some students to the school even though they do not attend their classes. Conversely, school may be attractive because it is not the adult world, which can be threatening and lonely, and which may offer no jobs or only dull, menial jobs even more boring than a dull classroom. An even stronger pressure to attend is exerted by parents and peers who urge the student to conform, by the promised rewards for school completion, and by the lowered status that accompanies dropping out. Although, as Ivan Berg points out, the prospects of dropouts are not without promise, and though more schooling is far from a guarantee of a good job, students are still faced with the fact that few attractive alternatives to school exist for a 12- or 14-year-old. If school is not a promising choice either, the student is in irresolvable checkmate. As a result, the majority of adolescents stay in school to graduation and beyond, even though little legal pressure may be applied on them to be there. For many schools and teachers, as well as students, the consequences of this stalemate are severe.

Imagine for a moment that the age of compulsory education is lowered to 14, and imagine that the other pressures to remain in school lessen: students do begin to withdraw. Who will they be? Gordon Cawelti argues that the children of lower class families would be the most likely to leave: parental pressure to remain would be less upon them than upon others, economic pressures to leave would be greater, and failures and disenchantment with school would tend to be more common. According to this argument, a vote for earlier school leaving is a vote for class discrimination, one which legislatures would not likely cast. With reduction in the required age, another set of arguments goes, the school will accrue benefits. Disruptive students not interested in learning will leave; learning for the remainder will improve, and those who leave will return when their motivation is greater. Cawelti is convinced that, as a result, high school programs will be even more likely to lack vitality, and that the prospect of large numbers of students ever coming back is highly questionable.

It is also argued that compulsory attendance regulations make teachers and the school legally responsible to act *in loco parentis* and thus force the school to be very conservative in its programs and very guarded in the kinds of experiences it can permit. By lowering the age of compulsory education, one also lowers the age to which the school has such custodial obligations. Free from these constraints, with a willing and voluntary constituency, schools will be able to create more vital, challenging, and compelling programs if they wish. But this argument is speculative. Where enacted law does not hold those in charge of the young responsible, natural law likely will. Some schools are already developing curricula featuring wide-ranging experiences in diverse programs of student choice. It is questionable whether the law restrains the majority of schools and whether with their legal bonds cut they would pursue radical program improvements. More likely, they are restrained by a complex pattern of attitudes, training, fiscal limits, history, and circumstances embedded much deeper than a singular legislative solution can reach or change.

Finally, lowering the age requirement in the state legislatures and the courts does not guarantee an effect on local
educational experience. As the Lawyers' Committee observes, "It seems obvious from our study that in most
states, the major decisions affecting the quality of a particular child's education are made not in the state capitol
but in the offices of local education agencies." Since the
laws of many states already provide mechanisms for exemption from schooling before the age of 16, an effort
to provide a greater range of alternatives for parents and
students could effectively begin with clarifying and widely
publicizing these options and directly negotiating with local
authorities to exercise them. If state regulations for curriculum are also clarified and publicized, then parents,
students, and teachers can more effectively argue for alternative programs which still meet the necessary requirements.

Altering the compulsory attendance law is very likely
not enough to change the present situation of adolescents.
As an isolated act it may be a retrograde step.

Opinions are divided on the issue. While a recent publication of the Institute for the Development of Educational Activities urges the reduction of required school
attendance to age 14, a recent publication of the National
Association of Secondary School Principals recommends
increasing the age to 18 years. Which course of action will
be most beneficial to students? To parents? To teachers?
To the states? What will the response be? And what side-
effects will occur? No one knows. While many opinions
and arguments are recorded, few facts and little recorded
experience can guide decisions about the rights of individuals and responsibilities of the states in matters of education. A number of groups have only recently begun to
study rights and responsibilities broadly and extensively
and to test them systematically in the courts. Further,
national discussions of compulsory attendance and compulsory education generally tend to obscure the fact that
we are really talking about fifty different sets of attend-

ance laws, fifty different sets of curriculum requirements, and many more different actual school practices in fifty states with their unique circumstances and histories of educational development. We are talking about changing the law for fifty different sets of circumstances, each of which should likely be considered separately to determine the most appropriate course of action.

This chapter has raised several problems concerning the correction of inadequacies in secondary education by lowering the age of compulsory attendance. First, reducing the age of required attendance does not address the other ways in which education is compulsory, ways which more tightly control the nature of schooling. Second, while the education arguments point out the need for reform, changing the law is a political process, and changing the interpretation of the law involves a legal process, both of which are based on quite different, more complex arguments and tactics. Third, each state legislates compulsory attendance and other compulsory education laws; changing them would mean dealing with fifty different sets of statutes and the circumstances in which they are applied. Fourth, changing the attendance law is not likely to change either school attendance or schooling very much because other forces keep students on the rolls and maintain the schools as they are. And fifth, a recommendation for a change such as lowering the required age of schooling should be based upon reasonable assurance that its effects will be beneficial. We have little evidence to base such an assurance on. These problems do not reduce the importance of the situation a change in the law is intended to improve, nor do they render a solution impossible. Perhaps a legal case against compulsory education as an abridgment of individual rights exists. The law can be changed by the political process. People can press for legal exemptions from school attendance as well as for changes in school programs permitted by the prescribed requirements. But individual choice of schooling and developments in schooling are more likely to occur if the problems of changing the law are addressed and if strategies are developed to more effectively counterbalance the power of the state over issues in education.

Recommendations: Information, Diversity, and the Right to Choose

The four major reports quoted earlier in this chapter argue that secondary schools, in general, do not provide for adolescents the kinds of experiences necessary for accomplishing the physical, social, technical, and intellectual tasks society requires for the achievement of mature adulthood. To provide these experiences, they argue, secondary schools in general must change drastically. The compulsory attendance requirement is considered one possible obstacle to such change. Reducing the requirement may be one means of freeing students to seek alternatives and of freeing secondary schools to create them. In the broadest perspective, the problem is how best to provide appropriate opportunities for youth to mature. Considering the complex issues involved in compulsory education and knowing they will not be swiftly resolved, the task force makes two kinds of recommendations: one dealing with the regulations of schooling, and another dealing with the creation of a coherent program of educational opportunities.

Recommendation 1: The age of compulsory attendance should be lowered to 14 in representative pilot districts, and the consequent benefits and problems should be studied to provide information on which to base decisions about this policy in all states.

Ready-made sites for these investigations occur in such states as Washington where the age of required attendance was recently reduced to 15. Others may become available in states where legislation for similar changes is apparently under consideration.

Recommendation 2: Detailed information concerning attendance regulations, forms of exemption from them, and procedures for exercising those exemptions in every

state should be compiled and widely circulated among administrators, teachers, students, and parents. For those who qualify, exemption has the same results as reduction in the age of compulsory attendance.

Legal exemptions from attendance requirements are more readily accessible mechanisms for early school leaving than changes in state legislation by which the requirements are set. The problem, as The Lawyers' Committee for Civil Rights Under Law discovered in attempting to compile state legal standards in education, is determining what regulations, exemptions, and procedures exist in any particular state. A coherent, well catalogued, and regularly updated summary of regulations and standards must be organized and readily available so participants in the process can study the laws by which practice is governed in their state.

Three forms of exemption are particularly worth investigating: proof of legal employment, completion of a certain grade, and achievement of a certain score on an academic equivalency test. If they exist in the state concerned, then accessibility of the exemption can be explored. If it is seldom used, then publicity may be required; if it is seldom granted, then strategies for increasing its use can be considered. One simple strategy, consulting state authorities, may be sufficient. California, for instance, has been improving its equivalency test to make it a more acceptable and workable form of exemption. Where such exemptions are not available, their use in other states may be precedents in a campaign for their adoption.

How widely these alternatives are available in practice is uncertain; access provided by local authorities must be investigated and tested. Unless they become widely used, exemptions will not effect school change as claimed by some advocates for a lower age of compulsory education, but they could give students legal options to school.

Recommendation 3: The law essentially determines educational rights and responsibilities. A communication

network should be established among groups and individuals studying the legal aspects of compulsory attendance, compulsory education, and related issues so that their efforts can be coordinated to provide parents, teachers, and school authorities a clear understanding of the arguments and the courses of action available to them in pursuing, through the courts, the changes they seek.

A number of groups have investigated or are investigating the legal aspects of compulsory attendance and other issues related to them. For instance, a project funded by the Foundation for Child Development at Yale Law School, under the leadership of John Simon, will produce an extensive interdisciplinary analysis of age-related aspects of education law, including the school leaving laws of the states. At the Massachusetts Center for Public Interest Law a study of the legal implication of changes in the compulsory attendance laws is in progress under executive director William Aikman. The work of the Lawyers' Committee and the National Organization on Legal Problems in Education has also included these issues in the scope of their work. In addition, such individual scholars as Stephen Arons from the University of Massachusetts Legal Studies Program and Howard Johnson from the University of Washington and legal advisors to state commissioners of education are studying these laws and their application. Such groups and individuals would all benefit from a regular communication network to coordinate their resources, findings, and efforts and to increase the effectiveness of their important services in clarifying laws on education, their effects, and approaches through the law to solving educational problems.

Two examples illustrate the potential value of these scholarly and practical services. The assumption that the nature of schools cannot be changed in major ways because of the laws and regulations binding them is untested—except by schools that do change. If these laws were clarified for school officials then their response would show the degree to which limitations upon their operations were real or imagined. Perhaps with a clearer understanding of the law and a court of decision other than the superintendent's or the commissioner's office, many could and would radically change their programs.

Such a league of specialists could also become an important instrument of curriculum reform by clarifying such issues as the balance between the parent's right to choose and the state's right to require the form of a child's education. Arons argues that *Pierce* v. *Society of Sisters* may be interpreted to require the state to maintain a position of neutrality toward parent's choice in schooling and to insure that state financing schemes do not place them in the position of abrogating that right to attain a free education. If that is true, then it may be argued that the state should equally support independent alternative schools which otherwise meet legal requirements and the desires of sufficient parents. If such decisions were handed down, the compulsory education laws would remain, but the conditions affecting all participants would be drastically changed, and as a result, schools as well.

Recommendation 4: A great effort should be applied searching for an appropriate set of alternatives to school, so that secondary students who decide not to attend have legitimate options to exercise, and for an appropriate set of alternatives in schooling, so that those who elect to remain still have suitable choices within the regular system.

Whether or not some changes in law will occur is uncertain: Legal cases can take a long time to be heard and decided, and implementing the decisions can take much longer.

Besides, changing the law may improve educational conditions for all participants, by permitting exemptions, for instance, but will not necessarily improve education itself. That task continues whatever the conditions. In the opinion of the Phi Delta Kappa Task Force, a broader definition of secondary education is required, one based more on service than on enforcement, more on opportunity than on obligation. The Task Force seeks a definition emphasizing the development of maturity and a form of education providing experiences and settings to cultivate the transition of youth to adulthood and a life of learning. It seeks a range of programs which enable parents and students to select from worthwhile alternatives in the way this transition is achieved. Within this broader concept of education, changes in the compulsory attendance laws would become enabling legislation rather than legalized abandonment. The task, now, is to attempt to develop that concept of secondary education and the pattern of operations by which it can be realized.

CHAPTER III

Secondary Education: Reversing the Dwindling Impact on Learning

Secondary schooling could be improved in many different ways, in pursuit of many different visions and models of excellence. But which of them should be chosen? Which form of education will best cultivate maturity? Which will have the greatest impact on learning? We don't know and can't find out for certain, except by developing and trying out new forms of education. But the range of choice can be narrowed and the process of development can be guided by formulating general assumptions on which to build a new model. While research, practical experience, and considered opinion must be examined, inevitably one must judge what is true and what will work best. The fourteen propositions that follow, therefore, are broad assumptions on which to rethink secondary education.

Proposition 1: Secondary schooling as presently organized and operated does not have a powerful, beneficial effect on learning that demonstrates it can educate adolescents with predictable results superior to other possible systems.

Major studies conducted during the last half century to identify the elements of schooling which improve student performance all seem to come to the same conclusion. When the powerful factor of socioeconomic background and the less potent but still measurable influence of the quality of the teacher are eliminated, it is difficult to show consistently that any change in curriculum, method, materials, or facilities greatly improves student learning, particularly learning as measured by standardized achievement tests. The Eight-Year Study showed students of progressive schools achieved at the university about as well as students from traditional schools and perhaps performed a little better in some other aspects of life. James Coleman's 1966 study, *The Equality of Educational Opportunity,* of thousands of students showed that changes in schools did not change student achievement. James Stephens summarized hundreds of studies with the statement that for every study showing achievement attributable to a particular method, another study contradicts it. In 1974 Harvey Averch and his associates concluded that research has not identified a variant of the existing system that is consistently related to students' educational outcomes. Even more confounding is the research showing a steady decline in standardized achievement tests and college board scores in the last decade.

Students who are taught tend to learn, but one form of schooling or one form of teaching a program is not demonstrably superior to all others, nor do improvements in elements of schooling appear to increase learning significantly. Several analyses (e.g., Averch, 1974; Jencks, 1972; Stephens, 1967) conclude that natural forces as well as incidental and informal instruction outside of school powerfully influence learning and tend to swamp the effects of schooling or scholastic achievement. These natural forces and incidental forms of learning may be one source of learning power worth exploiting in secondary education.

Proposition 2: The present educational system maintains itself and resists change. Major developments in education cannot occur unless major changes are made in the system managing it. To make changes in management, one must deal with the human, historical, organizational, professional, legal, financial, and political issues involved.

The forces within the educational setting which resist change are overwhelming and easily repulse, erode, or disperse the forces working for change. Some of the forces that maintain secondary school in its familiar form are these:

    a. Human: A few of the human responses against new developments in education are inertia, fear of the consequences of risk-taking, confusion in selecting the right path from among many alternatives, territorial imperatives about teaching subjects, anxieties about one's ability to perform in new ways under new conditions, and convictions arising from the certainty that familiar routines have fundamental rightness.

    b. Historical: Incumbents always have an advantage. Familiar patterns of schooling, though once experimental, by their very longevity have historical power to repel new ideas, which are usually rejected even before the first failure can give rise to an improved second generation. That which is, tends to remain.

    c. Professional: Education is the only profession in which everyone is trained by sustained exposure, though few are certified. Nearly everyone in America has twelve years to absorb one form of teaching, learning, and school. Many have sixteen years or more to absorb the pattern, while teachers in training spend additional years studying the pattern and practicing it under supervision before they can be certified to teach. The population shares one image of what education is. This image is maintained by the ongoing system. Teachers and professors usually assume that education includes the subject they were trained to teach; administrators, the patterns they learned to manage; students, the activities by which they have always been taught. The profession resists involving individuals without certification in planning and teaching, which effectively closes the system.

d. Legal: Public education is the only profession with an obligatory constituency. When law requires attendance, it is not necessary to consult parents or students, nor is it necessary to entertain their interests seriously and systematically. And when the law does not require specific results from that required education, the system does not need to seriously monitor its performance.

e. Organizational: To be approved, a change must be acceptable at each level of the education hierarchy and must require only a tolerable amount of reorganization of the school's complex patterns of operation. As John Pincus concludes, decisions in these situations are dominated by concern for bureaucratic safety and stability rather than the criteria of productivity and efficiency which prevail in the competitive marketplace.

f. Political: Schooling is a monopoly, but it is a monopoly whose performance is visible to several groups which either control it directly or influence it indirectly. Under pressures to meet often conflicting demands from state offices of education, state boards, parents, pressure groups, teachers, unions, students, and others, the bureaucracy tends to balance the pressures through compromises which minimize change.

g. Financial-Economic: Education receives more public

money than any other service except defense. This budget is spent with some requirements about what must be provided but without requirements to demonstrate results caused by those provisions, without regular external examination, without competition, and without any requirements by the system to pursue improved performance systematically or even to establish a procedure for that purpose. The financial factor, a powerful motive for increased effectiveness in other institutions, is not tied to performance and therefore tends to support the status quo in education.

h. Other: Other forces in the system also oppose change: the unrelenting pressure of numbers of students to be taught daily; the lack of time and services for planning change and recurrent professional education; parental insistence on schooling as they remember it; the lack of any constitutional procedure for developmental change within the system; and the number of vested interests such as publishers and the manufacturers of materials who benefit from preservation of the status quo.

Teachers, administrators, parents, students, or experts who attempt to change the nature of education in the face of these forces are heavily outgunned from the start. The recent history of innovation is rife with obituaries of their programs. To be successful, planners must be as concerned with developing strategies for confronting these forces of opposition as with developing plans for improved forms of schooling. Such strategies may include tying school budgets to implementing procedures for regular, systematic, planned improvement; compelling schools to compete for their clientele; and creating options to schooling for students well before grade 12. There is a ghost in the machinery of the school system resisting the development of education with a powerful, beneficial, demonstrable effect on learning.

Proposition 3: Schooling of adolescents is often conducted

in ways contradicting the nature and demands of human growth and development. Consequently, it loses power as a setting for learning. This power may be regained if schooling cultivates the student's ability to meet the tasks of personal, social, and intellectual growth—the universal curriculum of human development.

Secondary school practices often contradict the demands of adolescent growth. Youth is characterized by physical, social, and intellectual transformations which ideally culminate in the consolidation of identity and readiness for the transition to adulthood. Many school practices complicate those transformations and retard that readiness.

The quest for identity requires youth to develop autonomy, initiative, and industry leading to competence recognized as worthwhile by others as well as themselves. Such competencies comprise a wide range of performative abilities: athletic prowess, social skill, artistic accomplishment, practical know-how, technical competence, the ability to entertain, and many others, all of them useful and respected by the community. When the school narrows the range to theoretical, intellectual, and essentially verbal competencies, it denies to many students the recognition they need and could achieve in other circumstances. Worse, because only a few can earn success, many face the relative failure which diffuses rather than consolidates identity.

Learning is also less powerful when students are dependent in school, because growth demands autonomy; when students are passive, but growth demands self-directed action; when the teacher disciplines, while growth demands self-discipline; when students are isolated, though growth demands interaction; and when studies are largely abstract, but growth demands balance between the theoretical and experience and application in the world of adults. Not only will learning be more powerful when it meets the demands of growth in the adolescent stage, it will also prepare students for the challenging transition to young adulthood. The transformations of each stage and the transitions between them comprise a universal curriculum of human development. When education strives to cultivate and seldom obstructs human growth, it will have a more powerful effect on learning and a greater, beneficial effect on students' lives.

Proposition 4: Secondary schooling can more effectively educate students if it is more intense. It can be more intense by involving more of its constituency for more of its allotted time in educational activities which teach students what they did not previously know but can benefit from knowing.

Schools are low-intensity educational institutions. Many students do not attend; much of school time is not devoted to teaching; much that is called teaching does not instruct. As Diagram 1 illustrates, several factors cut attendance in classes, making fewer students available for active school learning. When dropouts are added to the number of students enrolled but absent and to the number of students apparently in attendance but not going to classes and the number of students marked present but released for activities unrelated to learning, the total number of actual absentees in the senior years for some schools, particularly inner-city schools, runs higher than 50 percent of the possible attendance. If they are not present, students cannot be influenced by school instruction.

If they are present in the classroom, there is little guarantee that the time will be spent in active learning. Many aspects of the classroom period seem to fill the time with nonlearning nonevents. As Diagram 2 illustrates, when all the regular, likely, and possible intrusions on class time have been subtracted, actual teaching-learning time is greatly reduced. A brief description of the segments in Diagram 2 follows:

  a. School Organization Time: Announcements, ceremonies, changing classes, circulating forms, assemblies.
  b. Classroom Organization Time: Attendance, announcements, directions, dismissals, excuses for

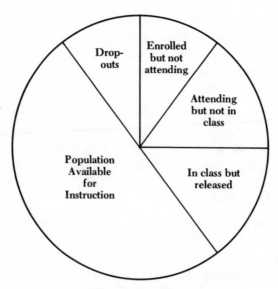

Diagram 1. The Reduction of Attendance in
Secondary School Classrooms.
(Not a statistical representation)

Diagram 2. The Reduction of Learning Time in
Secondary School Classrooms.
(Not a statistical representation)

bathroom, lost or mislaid books and materials, returning, giving, and collecting assignments.

   c. Waiting Time: Students waiting for a chance to speak, to have work marked, to have questions answered, to have directions clarified, to use equipment.

   d. Orientation Time: Settling down the class, laying out materials, getting students refocused and motivated, and starting the new subject.

   e. Distraction Time: Teacher disciplining students, student chatting or misbehavior, general maintenance of the curriculum.

   f. Free Time: Class amusement, games, time left when assigned work is finished, unsupervised time, teacher absence.

A third diagram could be made showing the kinds of teaching further reducing the intensity of learning. "Blind teaching" or teaching one lesson to a whole class without previous diagnosis usually leads to some being taught what they already know, many what they cannot comprehend, others what they do not care about or are not challenged by. In "teaching by testing," an exercise or activity is introduced, the class does it, and the results are marked. Because the activity is the behavioral objective, it is always achieved, though nothing new is usually learned. During "class talk" the teacher talks about the topic of the lesson or leads a whole class discussion about it. It is difficult to sustain at length, may cover the topic but contribute little to learning about it, and probably involves very few students for long. Under such methods the class may be attentive and busy, but the intensity of learning probably will be low. Learning can be increased by leading students more often to new knowledge and skill that is challenging but understandable and can be put to use.

Proposition 5: Learning situations become more powerful when formal studies are combined with appropriate concrete experiences and challenging productive activities.

The academic study of subjects or disciplines—the mastery of information, concepts, procedures, processes, and skills—is the basic mode of school learning in North America and is clearly an important one. By itself, however, it has an extremely limited focus encouraging misuse. The content of studies restricted to the classroom tends to be verbal, abstract, and theoretical and seldom becomes active, concrete, and applied. Any content which falls within the purview of the subject seems acceptable, whether or not it is useful to the student or necessary to the solution of important problems. Schedules and course outlines segregate rather than integrate content, which after the final exercise or test tends to be lost rapidly through disuse and forgetfulness. Most important, emphasis on academic study disregards two powerful elements of learning: concrete experience and useful productive activity.

Without complementary concrete experience, formal study is leached of sensory richness and many possibilities for learning. Formal learning without experience is like geography without a landscape. In the formal study of geography, one exercises the mind and learns to comprehend the abstraction; in the direct, concrete experience of the landscape, one exercises all the senses simultaneously and learns to apprehend the endless possibilities of the reality. The abstraction, while a useful partner to experience, is usually empty without it. Experience is synergetic—the whole is more than its parts, and much more than analyses of its parts—but formal learning about experience seldom is. All the studies of another culture cannot reconstruct even an approximation of the experience of being in the culture. All the analyses of a Shakespearian play in a book cannot replace the experience of attending a fine production, nor can ground training reconstruct the experience of actual solo flight.

But just any experience will not do. Just as there are strategies of formal learning, so there are strategies of experience. The basic relevant qualities are appropriateness, intensity, and preparation. The experience must be appropriate for the issue studied, to the student's age and nature, and to his present interest, need, or concern. An arbitrary tour of the post office is experiential but is likely to rank low as experiential learning. The experience should have enough quality or challenge to involve the student deeply. A shabby Indian show or poor play performance will be low intensity experiences compared to authentic Indian power dances or a performance by the Shakespearian repertory companies of Ashland, Oregon, or Stratford, Ontario. Students should be prepared to penetrate the surface and become absorbed in what they are experiencing. For some experiences this will mean preparation by heightening the student's awareness. For others it will mean guidance in examining, exploring, and manipulating as a specialist in the activity might—whether artist, archaeologist, or pilot.

Experiences with these characteristics put students in contact with the landscape of the senses, just as formal study enables them to go beyond the obvious and the easily accessible by working with the geography of concepts and theory.

Learning is still incomplete until a third dimension has been added to concrete experience and formal study. This dimension, often omitted in school though essential to mastery, is productive activity: applying experience and studies in an activity yielding a product of worth to the student—an idea, a song, a building, a critique, a garden, a pilot's license, or a service.* The stimulation gained from experiences and the insight developed from studies remain suspended and inert until one's own purposes integrate and apply them to some problem or purposeful task. Learning is incomplete until one has learned to use it. Much can be learned from the experience and formal analysis of plays, but the knowledge is consolidated, extended, and

---

*Raymond F. Moore (1976) describes evidence that large segments of school time can be devoted to manual labor alone, not only without loss of academic achievement, but often with improvement in learning, attitudes, and social relationships, especially if students and faculty work on projects together.

becomes usable when one acts in a play, writes it, criticizes it, directs it, teaches it, designs the sets, or makes the costumes.

But productivity is not desirable solely for its own sake. If the task and its result are trivial, irrelevant, of little use, or unchallenging, productive activity quickly becomes routine. The value of activity increases when it is personal, when one's own concern generates it, when one is committed, and when one's abilities and viewpoint are expressed. The process and the outcome should matter to the student. Value also increases when the activity characterizes the real world, rather than the school world, in problem solving necessary in life rather than in practice exercises. And the value for learning increases when the activity challenges, when it tests the students' ability to make ideas work, to overcome obstacles, to learn from mistakes, and to achieve the goals they set.

The question is not whether one should teach by experience and discovery, study and practice, or activity and productivity, but how the three dimensions of learning can be combined into a simple powerful method.

Proposition 6: Organized and managed so that their active socializing forces contribute to learning and maturation, secondary schools will have greater influence on student achievement. This can be done in many ways, including limiting school size and introducing more open organizational patterns to increase the range of opportunities for students to learn from adults and from each other.

Secondary schools have a powerful social influence on students, but it is often an unintentional consequence rather than a   planned effect of the program. Being in school separates youth from adults and youth of one age from youth of another. School is a social center for young people, but as a peer group society—created by age segregation—its purposes and activities often differ from those of the school. Large size increases the impersonal and bureaucratic nature of the school, intensifying the isolation of students and their resistance to the school as an institution.

If the purpose of the school is to foster the development of youth toward adulthood, it can utilize the considerable influence potential in social forces such as these:

a. The influence of the parents and the home on attitudes, expectations, beliefs, and achievement.
b. The influence of heroes and respected adults as role models and informal teachers.
c. The influence of peers in establishing behavioral norms, the local culture, and the expectations of that culture.
d. The influence of membership in a small group, in or out of class, which has developed group cohesiveness and common purpose.
e. The influence of intimates as observers, reflectors, and informants at the most personal level of experience.
f. The influence of the teacher as a knowledgeable adult, a model, and a guide in a position of power—particularly, the expectations communicated by the teacher to students about their school performance.

These forces can be utilized to cultivate learning, maturation, and appropriate forms of socialization. When traditional forms of organization give way to more flexible patterns breaking down the isolation of youth, the range of learning opportunities is extended and the range of opportunities for instruction is increased, enabling the teacher to adapt the program more appropriately to students. The following approaches can be considered:*

a. Organizing students in small groups as working teams for the duration of a challenging task pursued in the school or community enables them to participate with others intently, form relationships, and experience group cohesiveness and cooperative accomplishment.

---

*Most of these possibilities are discussed in detail in the Coleman Report (1974), providing background, explaining advantages and disadvantages, and reaching conclusions which are integrated in this list with others.

b. Integrating students of different ages into the same group enables the older to learn about the younger, to take responsibility for them, and to learn a subject by teaching it. The younger learn from new associations and from the individual teaching received.

c. Allowing students involved in individual self-directed learning to organize in flexible task-oriented groups offers them opportunities for support and for sharing problems, ideas, and accomplishments.

d. Bringing together youths and adults from the community for various shared activities in and out of school breaks down the separation of generations and enables youths to learn skills and ideas by informal as well as formal exchanges.

e. Organizing students and teachers in smaller schools (enrollments of 250 to 500) and autonomous units within schools makes programs more adaptive, groupings more flexible, and contacts more personal.

In such ways the social climate of the school can be improved and the social forces in the school can contribute more consistently to student learning and maturing. If the potent influence of the home and of respected community adults can also be enlisted to pursue educational goals, in a cooperative relationship with the school, then the most powerful forces—often untapped and uncoordinated—can help educate adolescents.

Proposition 7: Learning in the social domain which provides important interpersonal experiences, shared studies, and cooperative activities will enable students to relate to others better and cooperate with them more successfully. Such a program will be most effective when interactions in the secondary school and other learning situations model desirable forms of human relationships.

If increasing the range of relationships in school and providing opportunities to experience the adult role in the community are important, learning how to function successfully in those social relationships is essential. From the student's perspective, every class situation is a social situation. Every lesson inescapably affects him socially as well as intellectually or academically. He is learning each day whether or not he belongs, has friends, is liked, is safe, can work with others, has a desirable role, can share urgent but hidden feelings, has hope, is competent, and so on. While these issues are always active concerns of students, they are often ignored or, worse, exacerbated by the way academic learning is conducted. In either case, such a contradiction between student need and educational service further weakens the potency and long-range value of learning.

Social learning, as important as academic learning to the student, to the school, and to society, is generally ignored. Violence, divorce rates, crime, delinquency, mental illness, and corruption; local, national, and international problems in political relationships; racial and sex-role conflicts are widespread social ills, yet schools do little more than teach information about them. Senator Birch Bayh's recent report detailing the alarming increase in murder, rape, vandalism, extortion, disruption, and absenteeism in American high schools shows that these social ills are becoming more common among students as well.

Every youth must form intimate relationships, and many will form families and raise children. All will become citizens in whose hands the future of the smaller and larger communities will lie. All will become members of social groups, including service groups. Many will become members of teams, staffs, or boards in their work; many will hold jobs in which relationships with others is the work. All of these are necessary and inevitable futures for students; all require the ability to relate sensitively to others, to cooperate and to lead, to function productively in a group, to resolve conflicts, to oppose the unethical exercise of authority, and to work toward a greater social purpose than personal gain. Developing such abilities requires more than the dissemination of information. It requires exceptional social experiences, interpersonal skill training, and application in real social tasks. Yet few schools provide for sustained learning in the social domain. Rather, they tend

to create classroom and school settings which at best ignore the interpersonal dimension, and at worst demonstrate to students day in and day out the interpersonal
insensitivity and conflict which we, as a society, most ur-
gently need to overcome.

**Proposition 8: Secondary education will cultivate the grad-
ual transition of students from childhood roles to adult
roles by increasing their involvement in adult situations,
issues, tasks, and responsibilities.**

B. Othanel Smith and Donald E. Orlosky conclude that
an adolescent whose life is limited to a home and school
environment, sheltered from the social, economic, and
political functions of the community, does not confront the
activities, people, and institutions necessary for learning to
cope satisfactorily with an adult role. Schooling is an experience in discontinuity when students desperately need
to experience continuity with society, the culture, and particularly the tasks which loom ahead of them, around them,
and within them. Adolescent students are overpowered by
interest in and anxiety about their futures—their ability to
find their work and a job, to find a life partner, to create a
satisfying life-style, to earn the material rewards they seek,
and, perhaps, to make their lives matter in some way in
the larger scheme of things. At such a time, schools continue to teach subjects which have a distant and abstract
relationship to these issues and do little to inform them or
assist students in their resolution.

Similarly, though students can most benefit from align-
ing school learning and daily experience so that school demands interact with what students do on their own, the
school maintains its focus on academic learning, on
theoretical information, skills, and exercises conducted
within the confines of the school. Many argue that the
school diffuses its efforts when it attempts more. When
learning is not constantly used, and not integrated into the
individual's life-style, however, the loss through evapora-
tion may be greater than the loss through diffusion.

Again, when students most need to find out who they

are, what they can do, and what they might become; when they most need to explore those issues, test themselves and their ideas in real situations, and find confirmation of their capacities among respected adults; at such a time students are in school and out of touch with work, with real responsibilities, with testing situations, and with adult relationships in the community.

In these conditions lies the essence of the transition to adulthood, the gradual movement from experiencing oneself as a dependent, inexperienced, and uncertain child to experiencing oneself as an increasingly independent, competent, and confident adult. The young prepare for and accomplish this transition by interacting with adults and by practicing adult roles. Such practice is most effective when the experiences are real rather than simulated and when they increasingly challenge the student's ability to be an equal in responsibility, relationships, and competence. This forward and outward drive in the young is often confounded by anxieties arising from the isolation and passivity of school. When schools actively cultivate this transition, the drive adds force to the learning process, the frustration of adult bodies in childlike roles is reduced, and the demands of maturity are more likely to be met— with resulting benefits for students, the school, and the community.

Proposition 9: Regular training and experience in selecting, designing, implementing, and managing their own learning will enable students to become independent and will prepare them for a lifetime of self-education.

An important part of the transition from childhood to adulthood is the transition of power. For the secondary school this means the transition of teacher power to students' power to govern their own actions and to design and implement their own learning. Self-directed learning is developing and implementing a curriculum for oneself. It involves choosing, planning, and organizing similar to what the teacher or curriculum group goes through in planning a course. In addition, the student must put the plan into operation, handle all the difficulties which arise, and do the learning. This means a special kind of training, a kind of self-teaching apprenticeship to the teacher. And it means a different concept of resources. As Allen Tough discovered in working with adults on their own learning projects, it also means a unique kind of self-motivation, determination, and willingness to seek assistance.

Alvin Toffler, among many others, has said that a changing future demands the ability to adapt, to learn, and to continue to grow in one's ability to meet the challenge not only of changes in work, but also of social and personal changes. From a slightly broader perspective, participation in a learning community or society means being able to direct one's own learning as well as to learn in university, college, or night school courses. And from a still broader perspective, a person's life is the curriculum. Ultimately a person must be the self-directed learner who decides what that life program will be. By teaching students to direct their own learning as well as to learn what others believe is important for them to know, the school cultivates a new dimension of independence, the freedom of self-directed discipline, the fate-control of the confident act of self-will, and the hope implicit in learning to develop one's own potentials.

School is not a self-contained package. What matters in students' lives is not how well they have mastered tasks terminating with their school lives, but how well they have been prepared to function in the tasks of life. Beyond school the basic task is making one's own decisions, planning one's own course of action, and dealing with the consequences. Following the directions of others is important, but only after a rational personal decision to do so.

Proposition 10: Students trained to experience and direct their own sensory, emotional, and mental functions will be better able to achieve self-understanding, self-directed learning, and self-development.

Self-directed learning demands a kind of self-knowledge alien to most school programs. School is a crowded social experience in which the culture of the school and the standards of the peer subculture influence individuals. The subjects, the goals, the content, and the styles vary little for individuals, even in such individualized approaches as Individually Prescribed Instruction, Learning Activity Packages, Guided Self-Education, and Project PLAN. Though individual differences among students become greater throughout the senior years, the adaptability of programs to them is usually limited to course selection. Most schooling trains students to accept direction from others and to accept obediently even when the directions do not make sense. It trains them in the other-directed life-style described by David Riesman and his associates in *The Lonely Crowd*. The kind of self-directed learning described in Proposition 9, however, requires inner direction, the ability to make one's own decisions and to act on them. In the rush from exercise to exercise, laboratory report to laboratory report, when are students ever asked to be reflective, when are they ever shown how, when have they the opportunity?

While formal education has pursued its outer-directing ways, a dramatic and perplexing search has developed among the young—indeed, throughout a great segment of our society—to achieve self-understanding and self-fulfillment or altered states of consciousness. The array of ways and means is extensive, from meditation to religious conversion, from yoga exercises to alpha-wave feedback, from individual counseling to encounter group participation. This growing interest in the intrapersonal realm, this search for ways individuals may contact, experience, explore, and understand themselves and develop as persons, has become a quiet but far-reaching revolution.

How can the school deal with the inner realm when so much controversy surrounds so many of these practices, when so many charlatans mingle with authentic and competent practitioners, and when the problem is complicated further by the psychological dangers potential in some practices? Unfortunately, in North America we have few legitimized forms of training for inward experience and communication except prayer, and that is no longer permissible in most schools, even as a recitation. Some respected body such as the American Medical Association will have to approve some form of training for inner experience. Not doing so encourages indiscriminate practices and ignores an essential dimension of learning. Can anything be done in the meantime to meet this need for self-understanding, to offer yet another source of learning power to students, and, therefore, to education? The answer must be "Yes."

A number of personal, inner-related practices are safe, satisfying, and useful, and they can be learned. A few examples follow:

   a. Concentration: learning to attend, to focus one's awareness and hold it, to become absorbed.
   b. Sensing: learning to employ all the senses while experiencing an event.
   c. Visualizing: learning to form and hold visual images in the mind with increasing clarity.
   d. Imagining: learning to experience imagined events and to generate imaginative solutions to problems.
   e. Relaxing: beginning to release physical tensions and mental concerns, to achieve inner peace and clarity.
   f. Reflecting: learning to achieve inward concentration, to guide one's thoughts to issues, their importance, and their solution.

Perhaps now that meditation—the pacification of conscious mental activity—has been found physically, emotionally, and intellectually beneficial by researchers reporting in *Scientific American* and several other respected sources, it can be added to the list. Certainly, every person can confirm from personal experience that a center of inner peace where one can retreat, gather thoughts, let energies congregate, and allow decisions and directions to emerge is necessary. Self-directed learning depends on that ability and, it seems, the quality of one's life may, too. Possibly these skills of self-understanding are—as they are in many other cultures—the basis and beginning, even the purpose, of all education. All advanced thinking is reflective, whe-

REVERSING THE DWINDLING IMPACT 65

ther in the sciences or the arts, in problem solving or inventing. But it requires time and solitude, the opportunity and ability to step outside the crowd to hear one's own voice. And that is only the beginning of the challenge for schooling in self-knowledge.

Proposition 11: Secondary education, in search of learning power, cannot ignore the hours adolescents spend dormant before television and other media. This time can be used by cultivating student involvement in action programs, by teaching students to relate actively to the media, and by involving commercial television in the community's educational enterprise. Classroom television teaching is generally ineffective, but media resources such as video cassettes and video discs are flexible new resources for learning and teaching.

Classroom television will not revolutionize instruction. Teaching by closed-circuit institutional TV has not fulfilled its promise of twenty years ago because, as Frank Brown said in 1973, it tends to be little more than videotaped lectures without human presence or interaction in the classroom. Commercial media are too professional and too familiar to students for teachers to combat, using school media, and win out. But by emphasizing the active, interactive, and experiential modes of learning described in previous propositions, teachers will engage students in ways TV cannot, replacing audience passivity with participation in events and fantasy excitements with real challenge. TV contributes very little to human development; the numbing hours of passivity threaten it.

In the search for more powerful learning, however, TV and other media cannot be easily dismissed. If by the time students are 15 they have spent more hours in front of a TV set than in a classroom, and have spent many additional hours listening to radio and stereo, watching movies, and reading magazines, their total passive exposure to the mass media is staggering. Does this exposure influence attitudes, knowledge, and behavior? If educators are in doubt, business, industry, and political parties, spending hundreds of millions each year on advertising and programming to sell their products, certainly are not. Our lives have been irreversibly changed by the stimulation and information in both the medium and the message. But homogenized by ratings and the promotion of corporate images, programs usually do not stimulate mental processes.

At least four approaches may convert some of the thousands of hours of student media time to the purposes of learning and growth. First, time can be channelled into more active and challenging activities. Second, students can form more active relationships with the media by learning to produce their own programs, to select programs for their own purposes, to develop visual skills, and to interact critically with the presentations they watch rather than passively accepting their influences. Third, TV can be used more effectively when such flexible forms of programming as video cassettes and video discs are made as available to students as books. And fourth, the community can develop strategies for involving commercial television in public education so that business and the media share responsibility with the rest of society for pursuing valued educational goals, not through token programs but as the highest priority in all their operations.

Proposition 12: Secondary education will improve when the school uses the facilities, services, and personnel of the community; when the community uses the facilities, services, and personnel of the school; and when members of the community and school system share decisions about education with equal authority and responsibility.

The school can greatly extend its resources by using those available in its community and as far afield as imagination and organizational ability can reach. The community is usually rich in facilities, sites for a great variety of learning experiences, well-organized services of all kinds, knowledgeable people with something to teach, and opportunities for students to provide services and conduct useful studies. Similarly, the community can greatly extend its resources by making greater use of the school, its facilities, its personnel, and its programs. Both community and school can benefit from greater cooperation and interchange, by sharing decision making about purposes and programs, by sharing teaching services, and by mixing adults and adolescents in classes. The greatest potential, and the most difficult problems, lie in shared governance of local schooling.

Seymour Sarason concludes from his studies of institutions that clients and the experts to whom they give responsibility for some part of their lives—health care, care of the disturbed, or education, for instance—gradually become isolated from each other. The service becomes more institutionalized, more cloistered, more specialized, more professionalized, more convinced that only its experts can understand or provide its services and more resistent to outside observation and participation. In effect, members of the community become outsiders in the conduct of important aspects of their lives, even when lay boards represent them in the institution. This isolation is well advanced in education. Parents and the community have lost contact with the educational process, participation in their child's learning, and direct influence over decisions about what education should be. Much could be gained by balancing responsibility and participation between educators and other members of the community. In fact, such a balance seems essential if resources, services, and personnel are to be effectively integrated.

This union of school and community can increase the power of education in a number of ways in addition to the great extension and use of resources. By developing the purposes and program of education together, both school and community can proceed with new clarity and certainty, and can confirm new forms of education for students at home as well as in the field. When adults share learning activities with adolescents, they have a salient effect on the conduct and results of the experiences. And when parents share in education, they can more reasonably share in the liabilities incurred when students are on the streets, canoeing rivers, and working in factories.

The involvement of members of the community in an advisory capacity will not produce these results. A new pattern of governance is required in which school and community share authority through equal representation. School boards represent the community, and most boards have curriculum committees, but they are dominated by the expertise of the institution and seem most often to monitor programs for excesses than to exert leadership in this area. An education council broadly representing both the community and the education profession not only could make policy decisions, but also could deal with the complex problem of negotiating and organizing the extensive sharing of institutions, personnel, and other resources required by several of the previous propositions. Such councils could become an important source of grassroots decisions about the national purpose and the place of education in it.

Proposition 13: Secondary school systems can better create powerful educational experiences when they implement a process of continual, systematic program development that involves all participants.

Creating educational programs with greater power to improve learning requires a potent method of development. Traditionally, school staffs were analagous to theater companies trained and hired to present plays written or selected by state and district curriculum committees for a compelled audience. Their art was the art of presenting scripts handed to them. When staffs create theater events, involve the audience, move outside the playhouse into concrete experiences, and perhaps have to attract theatergoers who have other options, the art of presentation must give way to the arts of relationship, analysis, invention, planning, and organization. When a district moves from standard schools to optional alternative schools, lowers the age of compulsory attendance, creates schools within schools, or requires the traditional school to revitalize its program, it is assigning the task of development to school staffs. Unfortunately, their training and experience and the structure of the school are better designed for presentation.

The sustained pursuit of increased teaching-learning power means a transition to a process designed for systematically improving educational experiences. This is not a temporary device but a necessity for sustained renewal in the system. A process of planning and implementation includes such elements as:

a. Identification: Analyze students, teachers, facilities, and the program to answer the question, "Where are we now?" Assess all available resources, examine newly developed ideas, alternatives, and opportunities; generate a set of working propositions. Answer the question, "What problem needs to be overcome?" or "What opportunity should be pursued?"

b. Formulation: Invent the best possible program for moving in that direction. Consider all options until one begins to emerge as superior. Refine the idea into a conceptual model.

c. Development: Apply the model in the field. Evaluate the program, and on the basis of discovered strengths and weaknesses, develop the model through as many stages as possible, until it is a refined working system.

d. Communication: Communicate the program and results to others. Arrange for observation, participation, and training in the new program where appropriate. Begin another cycle of development.

During the last decade, systematically planned instruction—emphasizing goal ranking, specific objectives, and performance criteria—emerged as a procedure to achieve greater precision in teaching and accountability to the public. Although systematic planning makes operations and outcomes more precise, it can also more deeply entrench current practice and become a source of resistance to developmental change unless it is part of a process that questions what the school is doing and searches for better, greater purposes. The refinement of even more precise cer-

tainties must be combined with a systematic search for
even more promising possibilities, in what Ronald G.
Havelock describes as unending progress from what education is toward the way we would like education to be in the
future. This means establishing goals of aspiration embodied in a vision of what education could be so that change
is not confused action but a journey of development.
Several propositions in this chapter describe elements of
such a vision. This proposition calls for a procedure by
which it can be systematically formulated and pursued.
Few schools or districts have one.

**Proposition 14: New secondary school programs cannot be
successfully developed and implemented without creating a supportive setting which supplies the process, organization, environments, conditions, materials, and
people necessary for its success.**

A new process and the programs it generates cannot
successfully operate in old organizational structures. For
example, a setting designed to support teacher presentation of a set curriculum through assigned materials within
the confines of the school will conflict with a program designed for local planning of programs and development of
experiences occurring throughout the community. The new
program will fail from lack of support and open opposition. In creating a new process and new programs, it is
equally important to create a new setting in which the conditions, organization, and staff comprise a uniquely appropriate support system.

What are the elements of a supportive setting? Establishing a program to train students on the job in marketable skills requires the enlistment of skillful lay teachers,
negotiating for their time and use of their work sites, arranging liability coverage and union cooperation, organizing compatibility with the school schedule, matching
students and jobs, managing and supervising the program,
and more. Most new programs require such logistical
support as willing, capable, and specially trained personnel; appropriate new materials; suitable environments;

appropriate legal, financial, and supervisory conditions; suitable organizational patterns; and a process for determining and implementing improvements. The planners of new programs often have to deal with all of these problems themselves. If their exhaustion does not bring the program to an end, opposition from the established order often does. Program and setting considerations are inseparable.

Even when a supportive setting has been established, one complaint from outside, one problem, one unforeseen complexity, or one new necessity may swiftly end new programs. Mistakes in new ventures are seldom recognized as opportunities for improvement. More often they are cause for termination. How can support for new programs be guaranteed despite such normal difficulties? Seymour Sarason recommends that parties involved in the creation of new settings for new programs negotiate a constitution which clearly sets forth the roles, rights, and responsibilities of the participants at all levels of authority, the procedures to be followed, and the conditions to be created and maintained. Such agreements seem essential in education.

School systems have not been responsive in the past. How, then, can the process of development, an appropriate setting, and a working agreement between developers and educational authorities be implemented? Harvey Averch and his associates conclude from research studies that

> Innovation, responsiveness, and adaptation in school systems decrease with size and depend upon exogenous shocks to the system.

John Pincus finds that systems are not responsive because educational policy makers guard bureaucratic safety and stability, avoid external social and political pressures on the school, and seek consensus with peer opinion. Within these constraints schools tend voluntarily to adopt innovations which promote the school's image. Pincus describes several exogenous shock methods to increase responsiveness. The structure of incentives can be changed to stimulate change. Part of all grant money can go for things the school is reluctant to do rather than things it wants to do. Voucher systems, youth endowment plans, and open enrollment can be instituted to change the market structure of schooling. The locus of control can be changed by decentralizing decision making to the school level, to community boards, or to teacher-student governance. Whatever the choice, it seems that a system of development with an appropriate setting and a negotiated agreement will only be possible when legislation creates an exogenous shock changing the priorities within the school system and making systematic developmental change unavoidable.

Conclusion

Other propositions could be written on such topics as teacher education, the integration of secondary education with elementary and adult education, and equal universal educational opportunity. The Task Force, however, regards these fourteen propositions as essential considerations in specific proposals for the renewal of secondary education.

Many existing school programs illustrate one or more of the propositions; in fact, such programs as the ones listed in Appendix II first drew our attention to some of the principles we formulated. And many teachers actively pursue better conditions for student learning such as the ones described in this chapter. Still, the majority of secondary schools seem impervious to anything but the most cosmetic improvements, not because of the failure of particular people but primarily because of the circumstances dominating decision making in education. Those circumstances are created by all of us, academics and practitioners, administrators and teachers, parents and children, politicians and publishers, businessmen and reporters. If we share responsibility for what schools are, we share responsibility also for what they become.

The Task Force is attempting to build a vision of what secondary education might become by identifying forces which could benefit students and the community. That vision concerns what people can be if they are able to experience, understand, and act; if they understand themselves, can relate to others, and have developed intellectual and technical competence; and if they learn to relate fulfilling their own purposes to fulfilling the purposes of the community. It is a vision in which parents and other adults in the community share with the school the responsibility for providing an education in which these learning achievements are possible. It is a vision in which learning, conceived as an academic pursuit limited to formal courses, is extended to learning conceived as a life-style in which individuals continuously grow in their ability to experience, relate, understand, and contribute. We envision a revolution of purpose, action, and fulfillment through learning. We envision an educational system which itself aspires to such a future.

The next chapter reports on a school district with such a vision and how it developed an educational program embodying many of our fourteen propositions for the improvement of secondary education.

CHAPTER IV

Is Eleusis Community School the Model We Seek?

The Phi Delta Kappa Task Force on Compulsory Education and Transitions for Youth first became interested in the Eleusis Community School when one of our members circulated a report from the Carleton *Register* (September 25, 1976) in which a student, speaking to the local Rotary Club about a program for retarded children, referred to his school's constitution. Thinking of the revolutionary Bill of Rights printed in the underground literature of the sixties, we were surprised by this passage:

> The articles of our constitution called the Rights and Responsibilities of Students give us freedom to come and go from the school whenever we want to, after we're 14, but hold us responsible for reaching certain levels in a number of skills and for accomplishing certain tasks each year. One task requires us to form a team of five to ten students and then work together to identify someone in our community who needs help, and to provide the service they need.

Our team believes the retarded children at the Cedars spend too much time indoors, out of sight and out of contact with the community. So, with the help of Mr. Selwood, the resident psychiatrist, and Karen Parkins' father, we've designed a community recreation program for them. . . . We hope you can give us the thousand dollars we need to rent a bus pretty regularly during the summer to get those kids around.

The idea of a school constitution caught our interest. The emphasis on student responsibilities, as well as their rights, was a major concern in our own discussions. Voluntary attendance after 14, coupled with mandatory achievement, seemed an interesting variation on the compulsory education issue the task force had been charged to consider. And the kinds of tasks mentioned in the Eleusis constitution suggested that the school authorities had found a way to stimulate the kind of community involvement, student initiative, practical learning, and value-oriented preparation for citizenship we were seeking. We telephoned the principal—actually, the director—of Eleusis, Mr. Pelman, and arranged for two task force members to visit. It proved to be an important decision.

The school, we discovered in our morning tour, is not a single building but a collection of varied sites for many kinds of learning activities for differing groups of students and adults at various times. The Center, as the original high school building is referred to, is a clearinghouse for both staff and student operations. The main floor has been gutted to create a large library, resource center, and study space. The second floor consists mainly of classrooms converted into offices where students make arrangements for using many other sites for learning activities, and into study rooms for work in the basic skills, though computer training and several other skill programs are offered at nearby Carleton Junior College.

The consultant in the Work Experience Office showed us the files of all the places in town and in the surrounding countryside where senior students could complete their task in on-the-job experience. The year is broken into four three-month periods. Students can visit as many sites as they wish but must sign up for two work periods during their last three years. The selection is vast. Almost every business, professional, and community service offers on-the-job training and experience. We visited a trucking firm recently established in Carleton and found two students working in the office and four in the maintenance and repair shop. Why does the firm go to this trouble and expense? Mr. Pelman explained:

> It's not just community spirit, though that certainly seems to be developing as a result of the changes we've made in the last three years. We offer incentives to business, and we've tied them to participation in community education. No license is issued without a signed agreement to provide work for students, instruction on the job, and a rather vague thing we've called working relationships with adults. The state as well as local governments helped to establish and enforce this regulation on an experimental basis. Besides tax incentives, newcomers now find benefits in the pool of trained people they can hire from among our graduates. That gave us a lever with established business. And once companies began signing up, it became an act against the community not to participate.

Students conduct on-the-job studies of various kinds, assisted by a staff member from the school or the work setting. Some perform job-related background research or training. Some identify problems faced on the job, study them, and develop workable solutions. Others study closely the job they perform.

Post-elementary education is divided into the junior and senior segments, each of which can be completed in either two or three years. The senior segment involves self-directed study of a core of skills and a series of tasks in each of the following areas: service, work experience, imaginative expression, physical challenge, and query, which is a problem-solving task requiring research and field work. These task activities can be conducted in every available space in the community and, as at least twenty Eleusis students have apparently demonstrated, in any part of the world. In addition, a variety of short-term courses, workshops, and events are open to all members of the community. A certain portion of these activities are required of all students. For instance, all seniors are required to participate in one of the five-week interpersonal skills workshops offered twice yearly, and some may be required to return for a second session. Each year, all must sign up for at least five of the many cultural events—theater, dance, art exhibits, and musical performances—arranged in cooperation with the Carleton Community Arts Council.

A fairly familiar program of traditional courses is also offered for those who prefer or need more direction and structure. Our guides reported that the number of students in this category dropped each year as a "Can't you make it on your own?" attitude developed. Several courses continue to expand their enrollments, however, and three have had to offer more sections. The reason: "He (or she) is just a great teacher, and I'm interested in the subject."

In addition to the new task-skills program and the traditional program, there is a third alternative route to high school graduation called options. No matter how well planned, a program cannot embrace all the possible and desirable ways to learn, nor can it accommodate the diverse abilities and interests of all the people enrolled in it. To account for the exceptional person and the exceptional opportunity, the Carleton Educational Council developed the options program, which is run by a small committee with representatives from business, community services, and the school who are empowered to consider any student proposal for an alternative approach to the secondary segment or a portion of it. The committee has three tasks: to approve or reject the proposal, to determine credit toward graduation which an approved option receives, and to arrange support for the student where necessary and possible. One student, whose father was sent to Brazil for a year, arranged to study the language and culture. Another student, who became interested in computers while working on a skills program at the local junior college, arranged to take three courses in computer programming and technology. As a result of their performance, several students working on senior segment tasks received offers from their employers to do further work and studies. As Mr. Pelman puts it, "We want to be in a position to legitimize any opportunity for a young person to learn and develop. Our job is to facilitate, not to hinder." As a result, the committee is expanding so that it can help students identify the options they want and to find suitable placements.

The junior segment of the program is quite different but is designed to be preparatory for the senior segment. The overall plan is called differential schooling. Ms. Axeford, junior levels director, explained:

> Our junior high schools were the most disastrous and inappropriate schools in the district. We decided to break up the whole pattern of tracks, subjects, 40-minute classes, and seven periods a day. We weren't getting anywhere with them anyway. Going from the modern elementary school to that baloney slicer was the grossest culture shock of all. We wanted to increase the intensity, the duration, and the variety of learning experiences, so we divided the year into two-month blocks, gave each school or site a different focus, and required all students to attend all eight sites in as few as sixteen months or as many as thirty-six months. We also require a minimum of three training sessions in self-directed skill development. They are run concurrently with the other programs so that students learn how to learn the basics. They have to be able to function on their own in the senior levels. Many need more than three sessions. It's still a little shaky, but I think the ideas are coming, now that we've realized you really can do things very differently but as well or better.

During the day we heard both students and adults talk about the Wilderness Center, one of the junior level differentiated schools. Unfortunately, it was too far out of town for us to visit, but we learned it is a remote farm which the school board was able to purchase at a reasonable price. Initially, students lived in tents and devoted part of each week to converting the barn into a wilderness study center and meeting hall and to constructing bunk houses, two of which are now completed. Living in the shelters in coeducational "families" or teams, along with a staff member and a parent or teacher, students cook their own meals and plan part of their day together. The program involves anthropology, archaeology, geography, astronomy, botany, zoology, and ecology—all studied in the field. In addition, students manage the stock and mixed crops on the farm—from which they gain much of their food —and practice wilderness management and conservation in the uncleared acreage. These group activities provide a framework for more specific individual studies and projects.

One of the girls told us, "The scary part is when you go out alone for two days with hardly any food, and when the first night comes, and it gets dark and cold." Answering our questions, she revealed that she went out three times, even though only once was required. She said, "The first time I went because I had to, the second time to prove I could do it on my own, the third time to get away from the family for a while and straighten out some of the hassles in my head." Other outdoor activities include backpacking, canoeing, mountain climbing, and working with the younger children who come out for shorter visits during the week. While the community campfire programs when each family entertained the others seemed to be the most pleasant memory, the adventure challenge at the end seemed the source of greatest personal pride.

We visited the Center for Fine, Applied, and Performing Arts (FAPA) but could not see much because most of the students were out on introductory experiences with musicians, artists, actors, craftsmen, newspaper layout editors, sign painters, and the like, and the rest were working their way up what they called competency ladders on their own. As Ms. Axeford pointed out, in addition to the Center, students are using studios, workshops, and stages spread all over town. "We've got as many adults in this center as kids," Ms. Axeford told us. "This is the school they most like to come to to start over as students or begin as teachers."

In the Local Bureau of Investigations (LBI), students

learn the investigative procedures used by police, reporters, city planners, doctors, chemists, and other members of the community. The other centers in this pattern
of differentiated schooling are equally unique and divergent from familiar forms of junior high school: the
Workshop in Practical Activities, the Center for the Study
of the World, the Humanities Center and Life Skills Laboratory, the Institute of Advanced Studies, and the School
of Self-Guided Education. The last two actually are schools.
The Institute is for intensive academic study in one or two
academic areas; the Self-Guided School helps students
learn the complex system of identifying, planning, implementing, and evaluating their own program of studies.

We asked Ms. Axeford how they developed the principle of differentiated schooling for the junior segment and
how they decided on the particular eight programs of two
months each. She gave credit to Mr. Pelman and his knowledge of planning:

> He would not let us make any decisions until we consid-
> ered what he referred to as the universe of possible alter-
> natives. People wanted to get to work on the new school
> and got quite annoyed when he said the ideas sounded
> too much like what we were doing before without success.
> We spent weeks gathering ideas from other schools and
> inventing our own. Gradually a skeleton program started
> to take shape. Then our plans developed very quickly.

From the many things she and the others said, four
guiding principles underlying the program emerged:

1. The new program must be geared to the way children from ages 12 to 14 grow—intellectually, in personality, socially, and physically—and to what they need for that
growth.

2. The program must be designed to help every child
develop a competence. That means greatly extending the
range of possible competencies and the ways to achieve
them. Students still learn "about," but now the emphasis
is on learning "how."

3. Parents and the community at large must become
full partners with the school in planning and executing

the broad program, if it is to become appreciably more powerful.

4. The actual learning in the program and beyond is the student's responsibility. The program must be designed to convey this message to students and to empower them to learn in a variety of ways and settings on their own. The effectiveness of the program will be evaluated according to the success of students in designing and implementing their own learning.

We interrupted the tour to stop for lunch at the Lake Shore Winter Club. That is, we thought we were interrupting the tour, until we saw the number of young people swimming in the club pool or lounging in small groups around it. Martin Babitch, the manager of the club, joined us briefly. We asked him about the heavy use of the outdoor facilities, and he told us:

> We're a private club, all right. But Pelman and his gang really put it to us. They're a kind of benevolent Mafia. "More taxes, or greater use of the club in slack hours," he told our board. It's kind of a reverse on the protection money racket. Money was getting tight, and the community had to decide whether to build new athletic facilities or make wider use of the facilities around town. When the directors of the clubs, the recreation centers, the YMCA, and the present school facilities got together, we decided we had lots of areas, equipment, and people to provide social and recreational programs for all the kids in the foreseeable future. We might even benefit from sharing as well.

A minute later, he excused himself, saying, "Before Pelman gets me to keep paying members off the premises on the weekends."

Mr. Pelman told us that Babitch was the chairman of the Recreation Council and that, without him, he doubted if the territorial disputes of the various recreation directors could have been resolved. But with his help, apparently, all the facilities in the community—including some private ones—are now available to students for some part of each day. As well as recreational and social programs, the council has developed a range of training programs in athletics. All the high school teams but one are now Carleton Community teams.

That one team is the Carleton Capitals, the basketball team. Carleton is apparently "basketball crazy." The team has been a strong contender for the state title for a decade and won it in 1972. The Alumni Association saw the shift to community recreation centers as a break in tradition and organized opposition to the plan, using their members on the Town Council to spearhead it. Somehow their opposition became opposition to the whole recreational program. The Recreation Council overreacted with an all-or-nothing theme and, but for a last-minute compromise, the entire program might have been stalled or rejected. "We simply left the team at the Center," Pelman said. "Makes no sense really; there's no gym there. But all solutions are not logical. We have to respect their feelings and be flexible enough to respond. We almost weren't and almost paid for it."

Returning to town, we discussed the constitution and the process which produced it. "You can't imagine the mess our schools were in. Rising numbers of dropouts, falling achievement in reading and writing, growing unrest among students, soaring costs, increasing clamor among parents, and demoralization among the ranks of teachers. Something had to be done," Mr. Pelman said. "We couldn't go back to a traditional program and we couldn't go on with our disastrous, haphazard accumulation of faintly liberal innovations."

"Why not?" we asked.

"In the first place, there is no evidence that a 'return to the basics' alone will significantly improve overall educational performance. To most people that return means a return to the whole medieval caste system of traditional schooling. The price in loss of students, in class and out, and in punishment to a predictable half of those who remain and fail, would be too great. And we believe the exacerbation of the unrest which already exists among students who find school inappropriate would bring the final cataclysm.

"But the school had become loose. The major innovation seemed to be a general abandonment of the concept of excellence. Alternatives were added. Enjoyment became a primary goal. And generally we were pleased—gave the student 'positive feedback'—for just about anything he did—if he'd just come and do something. That had to change. If we don't want regimentation, we still want disciplined effort. If we don't want high anxiety, we still want rigor. And if we don't want intense competition, we still want achievement, excellence," he said.

"But if you were experiencing the malaise of so many other schools only four years ago, how did you come so far in so short a time?"

"We decided to eliminate adolescence."

Pelman's reply astounded us. The task force was attempting to adapt schooling to adolescence; Carleton was attempting to wipe it out. Our confusion was unmistakable.

"Let me put it this way: Schools encourage youngsters to remain children. They are sheltered, protected, directed, entertained, organized, and generally indulged in the great school as womb. The result, with a lot of help from the business community, the media, and home, is an extended childhood. School does not allow children to become adults; it holds them aside until they reach adult age and then drops them out. Well, if we're creating adolescent adulthood, we can change it. And changing it is what we're doing—not just the school but the community as a whole."

"But how?" we asked.

"First, we tightened the focus and opened up the options. If we were going to demand greater intensity, we had to find more legitimate ways for children to be successful. Then we went for longer periods of concentrated work in one area. From the beginning of the junior segment, the community made it clear to the students that learning was their work and their responsibility. We provide the best learning situation we can, but we as a community expect a payoff in their talent, in their ability to use it, and their willingness to use it for more than their own good. Instead of being sheltered, they are challenged. Instead of being protected, they are encouraged to take reasonable risks. Instead of being directed, they are challenged to direct themselves as much and as soon as possible. Instead of being organized, they are required to structure much of their own time and effort. Rather than being entertained, they are encouraged to create their own entertainment. We provide training and support for students, but the school is no longer a womb—or a tomb. A support system, yes, but only to sustain them until they are strong enough to cut loose. We do not serve their adolescence, we serve their becoming adults and do all we can to assist them in gaining that personal power. It's a generous-selfish act of community. Their power is our power."

"What is that power you speak of? It sounds military."

"No, no!" Pelman answered. "It is nothing more than the ability to learn and the willingness to act for the benefit of others as well as oneself."

The elimination of adolescence was a provocative concept, but the day was more than half over and we still knew nothing of the dynamics which transformed the old program into this new system which seemed to be operating successfully despite the magnitude of the change involved and the number of people whose cooperation had to be enlisted. And there was also the question of the skills program—how and how much?

When we returned to the Center, Mr. Pelman organized our afternoon. "Marsha McNaughton is the leader of the Center Council. She's the best informed and most articulate person on the subject of our brief history. I'll introduce you to her and warn Phil Peobles, the coordinator of skill training programs—referred to inescapably as STP around here—that you will be stopping by."

Marsha McNaughton quickly brought our discussion to the point:

How to conduct an act of conversion. That's what you're asking, isn't it? Well, if I censor the gory scenes I'd have

to say that an ornery group of parents—a large ornery
group of parents—brought education in Carleton to a stand-
still. Secondary education, that is. Complaining that costs
were going up and student performance down, they
threatened to withhold taxes, march on the school or the
state legislature or both, and keep their kids at home. The
Register got hold of it, blew it up, and just when it seemed
a bonnie fracas was in the offing, the board and the school
administrators agreed to meet with the parents. It was a
no-nonsense meeting by the time we dismissed reorganization of the PTA and a few other token gestures and
made it clear that there would be widespread reform or
nothing.

Pressure from the legislature, we learned later, helped
to make possible the chemistry that led to the new programs. First, a bill making education compulsory to age 14
rather than 16 was going into its first reading. Second, a
bill tying in quality control or demonstrated performance
with funding beyond the basic secondary school budget
was known to be in preparation. Carleton's problems were
regularly cited as evidence supporting the need for both
measures. The chance that regular schools might drop
severely in population and the threat of minimal funds
combined to make administrators, trustees, and teachers
anxious to find alternatives.

In fact, one of the "gory scenes" apparently occurred
when a committee of parents and representatives of the
teachers union confronted each other on the issue of direct community involvement in school decision making and
teaching. The president of the local is reported to have
shouted, "No way, no possible way! We'll shut the school
down first!" Although he cited union regulations, teacher
certification laws, and other evidence, he could not silence
the parents—particularly a prominent local lawyer, who
replied that if the teachers' union was going to stand in the
way of improving education, the community would have to
take them to court or go directly to the legislature. "The
schools belong to the community. We hire you to do a job
for us. We pay for the schools for you to work in. Now you
think they are your private preserve. Well, if we have to

fight you for them, we will. And we will win."

Marsha McNaughton went on:

> In this atmosphere, the commissioner of education dropped his bomb. Every secondary school in the state was ordered to produce a plan for renewal which would be the work of citizens and students as well as teachers and administrators. This process, he stated, must generate goals, and the goals must represent the community's aspirations, improvements in schools which all members can work toward together.

Under these conditions, the first community meeting was held. Two decisions were made which created the organization and the operating rules for the renewal of education at Carleton. The first was a decision to form the Council of Educational Leadership (CEL) in which the membership would be shared by representatives from the administration, the teachers, the community, and the students. This became the central planning body for educational services in Carleton. The second was a decision to write a constitution which clearly stated the rights and responsibilities of each group—with safeguards, checks, and balances—and described the operating procedure by which the process would function.

One of the teachers told us, "We realized that, if we were going to improve the quality of education, it would mean a number of changes. Those changes would be impossible without changing the setting. Without a redistribution of authority and responsibility, a new planning procedure, and a new sense of purpose and direction, little could change." After the constitutional changes, the meetings focused quickly upon basic skills, competence, practical skills, challenging experiences, active citizenship, and academic excellence as major considerations. CEL consulted experts, set up committees to bring forward recommendations, and gradually generated the three-pronged secondary education design: a modified academic program, the junior-senior segment competence program, and the out-of-school options program. That design was the key to

opening the planning process for real community participation. Ms. Axeford explained:

> We knew from the research that smaller units of staff and
> students are more flexible, more likely to innovate, and
> generally more viable as social environments. Our design
> created a network of such units, each with its own setting,
> staff, and students. We made each unit totally autonomous
> in developing its program, except that it must fulfill its
> purpose within the community network and must share
> planning with parents and students. With the numbers of
> people involved sharply reduced, with a much more fo-
> cused purpose, and with a staff unified behind that pur-
> pose—though not about how the purpose would be
> achieved—planning was much more intense and productive.

Two procedures clearly helped the units to plan efficiently.
One was the Planning Book and the other was an advocacy
procedure for presenting program proposals to the council.

The Planning Book identified the major problems to be
solved in planning a small school. Each entry stated one
problem clearly, identified the major options, discussed the
possible advantages and consequences of each, invited
other alternatives from participants, and suggested a basis
for deciding among them. Once the program and the organization were developed, the school committee prepared
a proposal for an open meeting of the council. Copies were
widely circulated. At the meeting two council members
questioned the committee, one probing the shortcomings
of the proposal, the other attempting to emphasize its
strengths. An empty-chair procedure enabled others to
come forward and question. But the emphasis was constructive so that the council could make the best possible
decision: either to approve or to recommend revisions. This
process, we were told, at once motivated and guided the
planners, and increased communication and understanding throughout the system and the community. The debates
were still intense, but much more pointed and productive.

Many problems of implementation arose, but the people
needed to solve them were usually represented on CEL
and so could provide the knowledge, influence, connec-

tions, and resources necessary. For instance, when the problem of cooperation of local business in the work-study program arose, the president of the Rotary Club formed a group of leaders to solve the problem. Carleton found it had the resources and the cooperation. The problem was to organize the program and to repay the service with useful help from students and some cooperation from the community. It was not so much a case of whether it was possible as how to make it feasible and operational. As Mr. Pelman pointed out, "We discovered that the resources for our programs are there, often already organized but in separate places. Our problem was pulling them together, organizing them, and using them intelligently, with some payoffs for the assistance."

While creating a pattern of schooling which challenges the young to reach out toward the limits of their energy, ability, imagination, and compassion, the people of this district moved school back into the community, and by that process have helped to regenerate the sense of community itself. As one secondary levels girl told us,

> At graduation, when everyone is showing what they've done, and the parents and teachers and younger kids are all around, you really feel like you're part of something and what you're doing's important.

It was an appropriate concluding remark on our tour.

By now, it is apparent that Carleton is a fictitious place, and the Carleton Secondary School program and all the people in it are imaginary. The reason for presenting this vignette is to help readers visualize our proposals in operation before they confront the more abstract, theoretical descriptions of them in the following chapter. Some aspects of education in Carleton may seem familiar. Several have been written about elsewhere, and many individual elements are already in operation in different centers in North America, giving the less familiar aspects of Eleusis an air of reality. But the Carleton model is far from a collection of unrelated alternatives. It is an attempt to integrate a number of developments into a new form of secondary education with a distinctive purpose, process, and context which will have a powerful, beneficial influence on the maturation of adolescents and their transition to adulthood.

Eleusis Community School is named after the temple city of the Greek goddess Demeter. When her daughter, Persephone, was stolen by Hades and taken to the underworld, Demeter devastated the earth and threatened to leave it dried out and sterile until her daughter was returned to her. Finally, the gods relented and permitted Persephone to return for a portion of each year. Demeter celebrated her return every spring by renewing the earth with fresh growth. Similarly, we seek the renewal and growth of secondary education, not just a major step forward, but a process of regular regeneration. Eleusis Community School and the Carleton School District represent the kind of education we are working to accomplish. The next step is to describe the theoretical model on which this particular vision is based.

CHAPTER V

Education as the Development of a Learning Life-Style

Many different programs can be developed from the propositions for the renewal of secondary education outlined in chapter 3. The program described in the following pages—the model underlying imaginary Carleton's imaginary Eleusis School—is proposed by the task force as appropriate for the education of youth becoming adults. More precisely, it is a conceptual model proposed in the belief that it can be shaped into a powerful and beneficial form of education.

Program Element 1: Education is a lifelong, continuous process providing the experiences, environments, relationships, challenges, and guidance individuals need to maximize their opportunities for growth in each period of personal transformation, to prepare for the changes demanded by each period of transition, and to cultivate

the ability to negotiate the demands of changing circumstances in the society in which they live.

The life of each individual is a life of transformations. Physically, intellectually, emotionally, and socially we are always changing, propelled by time through stages of human maturation. The life pattern may be divided into at least six stages, each with its own characteristics, requirements, challenges, and opportunities, each forming a necessary and influential foundation for the next, from the prenatal period through infancy, childhood, adolescence, youth, adulthood, and old age. The transformations of infancy, for instance, include rapid growth, developing perception, learning to walk, acquiring the basics of language, establishing some degree of autonomy, and generally creating the basis for future attitudes, self-concept, and behavior. Each period or stage has its cluster of unique, interrelated features.

A social transition—a change in role, activities, and expectations requiring new ways of functioning—often marks the shift from one stage to another. The infant leaves home for school, the adolescent leaves school for work, the middle-aged leave work for retirement, the old face the final and unknown transition of death. (see Diagram 3). The approach of each transition confronts the individual with new conditions but similar uncertainties about them: Can I meet the new demands that will be made of me? Can I function in these new environments? Will I be able to relate to those unfamiliar people? Inward struggle accompanies outward changes in circumstance as individuals attempt to redefine themselves in their new relationships. The moment of transition varies according to individual rates of maturity and the opportunities and expectations of particular societies, but the changes present major crises on each person's route to maturity.

This sequence of personal transformations and periodic social transitions occurs against a backdrop of shifting local conditions and world-wide events. Sanity, survival, fulfillment of potential, and the quality of life all depend on the successful negotiation of the problems posed by fluctuating circumstances arising often from forces beyond the individual's control. People will experience contentment or divorce, safety or catastrophe, employment or unemployment, order or chaos, peace or war. While such changes as technological advance, altered social patterns, and environmental deterioration can be anticipated, many eventualities cannot even be guessed. Negotiation, in these unpredictable currents of circumstance, requires the ability to comprehend the situation, plan a reasonable course, and follow it. In the passage from infancy to maturity the arena in which the individual must conduct these negotiations gradually expands from the cradle to the community to the world. Successful negotiation therefore challenges changing individuals to accomplish workable relationships with a changing society on an ever-expanding stage of awareness and action.

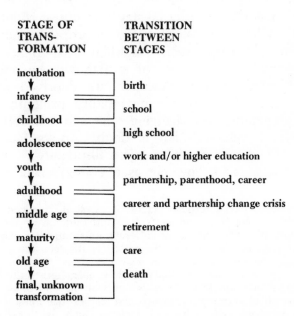

Diagram 3. Periods of Transformation and the Transition Between Them.

The learning most important to the lives of individuals and to the well-being of society is learning to accomplish the transformations, negotiations, and transitions of the universal curriculum, the tasks of human development.* From this perspective, education strategically organizes experiences to cultivate the various aspects of growth. Appropriate experience may be drawn from the full range of human activity—events, relationships, challenges, training, and so on—but to be appropriate, the priorities in educational practice will be designed to meet the priorities of the student's particular stage of growth. The requirements for mastering the structure of a discipline, for instance, are superceded, but not replaced, by the demands of development.

Because the curriculum of development changes throughout life, the need to learn is constant, sustaining the value of education undiminished throughout all stages of growth. The provision of appropriate educational opportunities is equally important for each of the ages of man. If education should occur at all stages of life, it should also differ at each stage. Without the appropriate nutrition, stimulation, challenge, social interplay, experience, and guidance, the transformations of growth will be retarded. Infants divested of such education are deprived beyond the help even of the best compensatory programs later. Without preparation for changing roles and self-definition, a successful transition is left in doubt. Adults facing retirement, old age, or death are often ill-prepared for these transitions and suffer severely as a consequence. And in

---

*Every individual passes through stages of physical, intellectual, and psychosocial development, but the nature and duration of the stages can be markedly different under different environmental, especially cultural, conditions. For instance, the nature of the teen-age years differs radically between a culture in which children often marry and work at 13 to 16 and one in which children characteristically remain in school until they are 16 to 26 years old. Cultural and other factors also apparently contribute to earlier and earlier maturation of the young in technologically advanced societies such as those of the United States and Canada. The concept of universality in the developmental curriculum must be tempered according to such variables.

their isolation too much experience, skill, and time are wasted. Without ability to learn new skills, behavior, attitudes, and tactics, individuals will have difficulty both in meeting the exigencies of changing times and in influencing them. Future shock, as even highly trained people in disappearing or radically changing vocations have discovered, is an inescapable consequence of our culture.

Program Element 2: The purpose of education is to assist individuals to create a learning life-style with a developmental perspective based upon the discovery and continuing refinement of each person's unique capacity for personal growth, relationships with others, and functional competence.

Education designed as a continuous lifelong process requires an approach to teaching and learning suitable for such a long-range perspective. If education is designed as resources for development—a strategic array of experiences, activities, relationships, and training to supplement normally available resources for growth—then learning must involve the desire and ability to use them. If transformations, negotiations, and transitions are the guidelines for a life curriculum, then the way to master that curriculum may be considered a learning life-style in which making full use of the resources available is a central ability. Teaching may be thought of as the cultivation of that ability.

What are the characteristics of education for a learning life-style? The most important seem to be cultivating a developmental rather than a static or regressive approach to life, instruction which is continuous with the ways people normally learn, skill in deciding for oneself and designing one's own programs of activities, and developing a pattern of activities which is challenging and unique in suiting each individual's growth.

In the regressive stance individuals ignore, deny, or reject opportunities for growth. Fearing the risks of change—loss of status, failure, personal suffering, or simply inconvenience—the individual retreats to once familiar practices and seeks sanctuary in an earlier time of life or history regarded as better and more worthwhile. Those who maintain a static stance—a difficult task in times of dramatic personal or social upheaval—maintain an indifferent, passive attitude toward inner and outer events, accepting whatever occurs with a sense of helplessness or a desperate clinging to the usual and familiar. From the developmental stance, individuals recognize and are willing to explore the changes in themselves and their opportunities. They are active rather than passive, experimental rather than conservative, risk-taking rather than clinging to the safe and familiar, and they change through growth rather than regression. Learning as a life-style is a developmental stance toward the transformations, transitions, and events in one's life.

A learning life-style is not restricted to particular times and places. Learning does not cease when the young leave school to walk alone, take a trumpet or karate lesson, meet friends, go to work at a hotel, or visit a grandparent. If learning in educational programs is continuous with the manner in which one learns from experiences, studies, and activities outside school and throughout life, it will be more appropriate for cultivating a learning life-style. One main aspect of continuity is self-direction in the choice, planning, and execution of educational activities. Education viewed as a lifetime activity is, and will be, self-directed. While individuals face similar transformations, transitions, and negotiations, the way in which they are met will differ. Everyone shares the need for a stable sense of identity, for instance, but the competencies on which it is based and the manner in which those competencies are achieved will be as unique as the identities themselves.

Developing a learning life-style means no less than designing one's own life. With this ability one can better experience the present with confidence and take some of the shock out of the future. The program outlined in this chapter is concerned with teaching adolescents so they will develop a learning life-style for lifelong education.

Program Element 3: Secondary education programs should

cultivate such transformations as independence and responsibility in behavior and the formulation of a sense of identity based on competence. They should prepare the young to make the transition to such characteristics of adulthood as the ability to apply their knowledge and talent in useful work and jobs, to act cooperatively with many, and to form loving, mutual, and lasting relationships with a few. Secondary programs also should prepare students to negotiate unprogrammed events in actual circumstances so that they will be able to cope with reality, give shape to their own lives, and participate in the evolution of society.

The transformations of adolescence occur at various times and varying rates and in diverse ways between the ages of 10 and 20. They seem to include:

1. Sexual maturity and increasing heterosexual interests.
2. Rapid physical growth and achievement of physical abilities roughly approximating those of adults.
3. Maturity of intellectual capacities, particularly in dealing with abstract concepts, roughly approximating those of adults.
4. Displacement of fantasies with realities. The need to know the truth about things and to eliminate fears, myths, misinformation, and illusions about oneself and the world.
5. Increasing desire for independence, for emancipation from parental control and the domination of other adults—a need essentially for emotional independence.
6. The need for self-esteem established through recognition of one's worth by others.
7. The need to achieve a sense of identity—a self-image—based upon a competence which can be pursued with initiative and industry and which foreshadows the kind of roles the young person can and will play in life.
8. The need for intimate relationships, affection, con-

firmation, and support from others, particularly
peers.
9. The development of a personal philosophy of conduct and life which enables the young person to
   consolidate values, make moral judgments, and deal
   with the unknowns of life.
10. Intense concern about the future: a career, a life
    partner, the state of the world, the individual's
    ability to cope and to be successful.
11. The need to learn, to achieve accomplishments of
    real value, to become consciously self-actualizing.
12. The need to experiment with the early evidence of
    adulthood: a driver's license, responsibilities,
    alcohol, child care, semipermanent heterosexual re-
    lationships, involvement in community issues, and
    so on.

Other transformations occur during the adolescent stage,
and all of those mentioned will not predominate in the
lives of all young people. Adolescents must deal also with
the backwash of incomplete or recurrent transformations
from previous periods in their lives and with consolidating
gains made in the transition from childhood.

Most important, they must prepare for the new roles
which will be demanded of them in their transition to
adulthood. These are basically the demands of growth
from immaturity to maturity and include changes:
1. from childhood dependence to adult autonomy;
   from low status with few rights to full adult status;
   from limited responsibility to major responsibilities.
2. from a relatively unskilled state to a competitive
   competence in performance in at least one or a few
   activities recognized by the individual and others
   as worthwhile.
3. from hobbies to work, from chores to jobs, from
   casual employment to life-central vocations.
4. from being looked after to looking after oneself;
   from using someone else's goods and environment
   to selecting, purchasing, and caring for one's own.
5. from being someone's child to being someone's

     partner, and perhaps to caring for one's own child.

6. from present behavior and a future course most strongly influenced by others to behavior and a future designed primarily by oneself.
7. from participation in society largely as a recipient to participation largely as a contributor.
8. from a narrow range of long-standing friends and relatives to a much broader range of relationships, many changing rapidly; from a singular life-style to a choice of life-styles.
9. from mandatory learning directed by others to optional learning selected and directed by oneself.
10. from local, surface understanding of the world and one's influence in it to far-ranging and abstract understanding of the world, with great responsibility for, and possibly great influence on, events occurring in it.

While many of these aspects of transition are inevitable for most young people, some are only possible. All of them will be achieved to differing degrees depending upon the circumstances and the person involved.

    Negotiation, for the adolescent, is learning to cope, the ability to deal with events and circumstances which lack formulated responses, and therefore, clear-cut training. How do we negotiate the situation if we are caught in a riot, if our parents separate, if we fall in love for the first time, or if we are hired for a complex job and are untrained? Most of human experience falls into this category. Individuals in such circumstances must know the art of coping, and they learn to cope by experience. Only by experience can one learn to take the initiative; to assess what is happening, generate alternative courses of action, choose, and act. From success—or at least survival—comes the confidence necessary for initiating further action. Abstract, classroom problem solving is a useful beginning but is insufficient to develop the art of coping. One needs a past rich in successful encounters with reality to bring to bear on the present and future.

    Development is a continual journey into the unfamiliar.

But one can learn to plot one's journey, to plan possible courses of action in light of anticipated conditions while remaining ready to adjust in light of unanticipated ones. Developing personal programs of learning with responsibility for both benefits and consequences is, therefore, a necessary part of learning to cope. But one does not always struggle just to cope. Alvin Toffler advises learning to consider possible and probable futures and to choose desirable ones to pursue. By such means we can anticipate circumstances, determine a preferable course of action, and act now to make that desired future more likely. In such ways we are better able to give direction to our lives, and equally important, people so trained and experienced can better participate in the development of society. Negotiation, in its fullest expression, means transcending preparations for one's personal survival to act for others in this generation and the next. Training for coping is best started at the beginning of life, but in adolescence the readiness to cope with realities of adult life must be matched with the opportunities and guidance to do so. Failure in this makes prolonged adolescence a creation of educational institutions.

Secondary education should be designed to assist students in accomplishing the transformations of adolescence, to prepare them for the social transition to adulthood, and to initiate them in skillful negotiations with the complex, unpredictable circumstances encountered throughout life.

Program Element 4: To cultivate transformations and prepare adolescents for transitions and societal change, learning situations should give full attention to personal and interpersonal as well as academic content. The treatment of content in each domain should be as concerned with intense firsthand experiences and challenging productive activities as with relevant theoretical studies.

What kind of events should appear in a program designed to cultivate transformations, transitions, and negotiations, and to guide students into a learning life-style appropriate for lifelong education? Mastering information, abstract concepts, and procedural skills through directed classroom studies is too limited an experience and the school too restricted a setting for accomplishing such an assignment. The program of events must deal more directly with personal and social issues and must involve students more in concrete experiences and the applications of learning and talent in challenging activities.

Learning situations more appropriately cultivate human development when the content is drawn as much from the personal and social domains as from the academic domain presently emphasized in schools, and when the mode of learning involves concrete experience and practical productive activities as much as the theoretical studies most common currently in formal education. That is, study in the academic domain common in schools should be extended to include experience, study, and productive activity in the personal, social, and academic domains of content.

The impersonal or academic domain of content involves the facts, concepts, skills, and products of familiar subjects and disciplines of knowledge. The interpersonal or social domain includes learning about others, from others, and with others; about forming relationships, resolving interpersonal issues, working in groups, and relating to others in families, communities, nations, and the world. Likely the most important of all, the personal or individual domain involves learning about ourselves—who we are, what we value, what we can learn and do, how to realize those potentials, and what directions we will pursue. Each individual's idea of what a community should be like expresses one's unique personal experience and perception. These personal concepts are tested and formed by interaction with others concerning community issues. What a group or team decides and does will be an expression of the individuals in it, their agreed-upon perspective often differing from the specific perspective of any individual in the group. Both the personal and the social perspectives on community issues expressed in this instance may differ considerably from the theoretical, academic perspective expressed in models of political, legal, and social analysis. All three domains are crucial and complementary in cultivating unique individuals capable of negotiating personal viewpoints in social situations from an increasingly rational and informed perspective. The task of education is not to superimpose the academic domain upon the personal domain using the socializing forces of the interpersonal domain, but to cultivate growth in all three domains using the power of interaction among them. Diagram 4 summarizes the kinds of learning in each domain.

Learning that cultivates development in each domain is a cycle including the sensory input of concrete experience, the process of theoretical studies, and the output of productive activities. Without concrete experience, studies

	Personal Domain	Social or Interpersonal Domain	Academic or Impersonal Domain
Learning by Experience:	Experience of one's self and one's personal experience of the world. Sensing: Responding	Experience of being in the group and experiences created and shared by the group. Interacting: Sharing	Experience of other's ideas, works, and ways of doing things—experience of the culture. Exploring: Manipulating
Learning by Study:	Study of one's self and one's own studies of the world. Concentrating: Organizing	Study of the group and studies of the world conducted by the group. Analyzing: Debating	Study of accepted content and methods: Studies of the world by experts. Comprehending: Practicing
Learning by Productive Activity:	Creating one's own ideas and objects. Imagining: Inventing	Negotiating a group goal and achieving it. Deciding: Cooperating	Generating one's own arguments and procedures. Formulating: Performing

Diagram 4. The Kinds of Learning in the Situation.

are disembodied. Experience provides the raw material, the full sensory input which can inform us, stimulate our curiosity, or move us to care about a subject of interest. In study, an orderly pursuit of knowledge and skill beyond the familiar and easily apprehended, one processes experience, gains access to the distilled experience of others, and accumulates an organized body of concepts and skills to apply to a broad range of unfamiliar situations. But experience and study are often of limited value, retained briefly, and meaningless to the student if they do not lead to output, to application, to productivity, to creation, to demonstrable value for living in the world. In productive activity, applying what they have learned in real and useful ways, students make experience and study their own, relate it to reality, and apply it to their own growth. When a person is responsible for applying and executing, it also becomes an act of self-discovery and a demonstration of oneself to others. Observing salmon ascending river rapids to spawn enlivens interest in the study of life cycles and the technology of fish ladders. But learning is embedded in life's events when such experiences and studies are applied in a job with the Department of Fisheries or in an action program to campaign for guaranteed waterways during local dam construction.

Because properly, and most powerfully, learning extends a person's unique way of comprehending the world rather than superimposing on it, the most appropriate starting point seems to be organizing and pursuing personal programs. Such self-direction is a necessary outcome of secondary education leading to lifelong learning. But experience, study, and productive activity in the social domain are equally important, particularly if the potent forces of relationships can be enlisted for the benefit of learning. In the small group individuals can test their personal perspectives, learn from others, master the process of working productively together, and deal with some of the interpersonal issues dominating the teen-age period. Also, when work in the academic domain complements learning in the personal and social domains, and concrete experience and useful activity enrich learning, it will be more important to students and more likely to have long-range, as well as immediate, value in their lives. The kinds of activities involved in this expanded view of educational situations are summarized in Diagram 5.

The categories in this model are descriptive rather than definitive. They overlap. Sometimes one aspect, such as the experience of a concert, is an end in itself. In many situations, such as building an engine, several categories collapse into a single activity. But they do represent more fully the range of ways people learn, and therefore constitute promising guidelines for teaching a learning life-style. They offer more suitable cultivation of transformation, transitions, and negotiations and thus constitute a more desirable framework of education for human development than familiar forms of classroom learning limited to study in the academic domain.

Program Element 5: Secondary education should be organized to teach students to develop and implement their own personal programs, to develop programs in cooperation with others, and to pursue appropriate programs designed for them. In this process teachers should be organizers of suitable experiences, environments, and personnel as well as programs of study, and they should be competent in methods of guiding individual development, training groups in interpersonal relationships, and teaching the skills of academic mastery.

All events can and do teach. A moment of solitary reflection, a vivid dream, a theater performance, encountering an unfriendly gang, meeting an admired adult, a death in the family, reading a book, achieving a new level of basketball control or performance on the French horn are the kinds of spontaneous teaching events which occur throughout any day. The task of instruction in a learning life-style is to train students to gain from these constant bombardments of stimuli and to make use of them, as well as more structured opportunities, for their own education. Designing

	Personal-Individual	Interpersonal-Social	Impersonal-Academic
Experience	solitude, encountering things, encountering self, awareness, imagining, becoming absorbed, trying new activities, exposure to new environments and conditions, experiencing new states of being.	encountering others, encountering self through others, experiencing relationships, roles, responsibilities, experiencing other families, races, cultures, sharing, caring for and being cared for, contributing.	manipulating object of study, attending and participating in performances (plays, concerts, vocations, customs), trying out and exploring, direct observation, simulations, reconstruction of other's experiences and procedures, experimentation, trying jobs and professions.
Study	increased attention, concentration, introspection, reflection, exploration, inner dialogue, decision making, planning, value clarification, inner imagery, identification of personal resources, management of growth, organizing studies on one's own, active learning, field studies.	learning to communicate, monitor group process, give and receive feedback, organizing to set and achieve goals, relating with warmth, genuineness, and empathy, training in relationship skills, implementing group study programs and activities.	imitating, absorbing ideas and practices from others (books, lectures, conversations, learning packages, other media), practicing for mastery, organized inquiry and formal experimentation, researching, developing frameworks and models, synthesizing.
Productive Activity	creating ideas and objects of all kinds, inventing, interpreting, hypothesizing, construction, building of all kinds, organizing something for a purpose, teaching others.	generating ideas, cooperating to serve selves and others, and to entertain selves and others, cooperating in community action programs, solving problems, challenging capacity of group, conducting cooperative exploration and research.	thinking to conclusions, evaluating hypotheses, formulating opinions and arguments, applying one's ideas and judgments, solving problems; developing new approaches, concepts, theories, practices, techniques, processes, and materials, performing in jobs, professions, career activities.

Diagram 5. Events in the Learning Situation.

learning situations extended well beyond academic studies in classrooms and merged with real life experiences requires an extended concept of instruction. Three central aspects of that concept will be discussed: the controlling principle for selecting and ordering educational events, the methods of instruction for guiding students through the learning events, and the contexts or environments in which the events will most productively occur.

In the traditional school the principle controlling selection from all possible learning events is usually necessity for mastering assigned subjects and disciplines. In developing a learning life-style the prior consideration is necessity for meeting the demands of the transformations, transitions, and negotiations in human development. The structure of subjects and disciplines continues to play an important part in the organization of academic studies but even in this aspect may sometimes give way to other, more suitable, controls. Usefulness in the execution of a productive activity, for instance, may guide the selection of academic content rather than organization designed for complete mastery of the subject. A student may be directed to particular areas of knowledge and expertise at different times for different reasons. Selection and organization will often be governed by such spontaneous purposes.

Each of the three domains of the learning situation gives rise to secondary principles of selection and design. In the personal domain students learn to select and structure their own educational program. In the interpersonal domain they learn to select and structure events and programs in cooperation with others—their juniors, peers, teachers, or other adults. In the academic domain students are directed to experiences, training, and activities others consider important for their particular development, programs selected or organized for them. Even in this domain, however, the teacher gradually transfers choice to students, so that they are able to seek out and utilize suitable structured events, programs, and activities as part of the learning life-style they will continue when they are no longer involved in secondary education.

The programs students experience and teachers cultivate may be thought of as various routes of progress
through a learning grid of experiences, studies, and productive activities in the three domains. In the early years
and in the beginning of most programs the teacher designs
the routes of progress, but always according to the controlling principle that effective design trains students and
groups of students to successfully map their own. One example of opening moves on a learning grid for an arts program is outlined in Diagram 6. At the beginning, a range

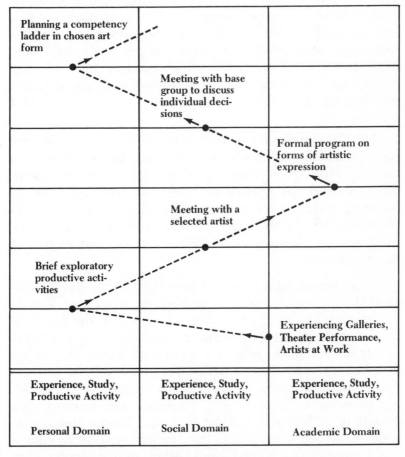

Planning a competency ladder in chosen art form		
Meeting with base group to discuss individual decisions		
		Formal program on forms of artistic expression
	Meeting with a selected artist	
Brief exploratory productive activities		
		Experiencing Galleries, Theater Performance, Artists at Work
Experience, Study, Productive Activity	Experience, Study, Productive Activity	Experience, Study, Productive Activity
Personal Domain	Social Domain	Academic Domain

Diagram 6. One Possible Route Through the Learning Grid for
a Program in the Arts.

of learning events provides an overview of the area of study and exposure to new alternative choices the student may later make. But range should gradually give way to depth so that the learning events become organized to increase competence in a specific area. The learning grid should become a competency ladder, a series of events through which the student plans to achieve a specific level of performance in a particular productive activity. For this purpose the principle of design is to cultivate interest into absorption and practiced skill into mastery. The ladder begins describing the performance the student aspires to and a planned sequence of experiences, studies, and activities for achieving it, and concludes with a demonstration of accomplishment. Each competence sought may be different in kind, each level of mastery pursued may be different in intensity. The controlling principle is teaching students to design and climb the competency ladder on their own.

The "present-practice-test" method of instruction still most common in schools is inadequate for conducting a range of educational experiences in such varied sequences. Diverse programs require a variety of techniques in organizing, guiding, leading, and directing. Techniques appropriate for training and guiding students in each domain can be summarized as shown in the chart at top of following page.

These broad categories of instructing techniques are expanded into sixteen specific methods in *Models of Teaching,* an excellent analysis by Bruce Joyce and Marsha Weil. To function in diverse learning situations teachers must be capable of such varied forms of instruction. But rather than being the continuing performer of educational events, the teacher will often be a broker arranging and organizing experiences, people, and resources for learning and consulting with students about their use. Rather than translating provided curriculum, the teacher will plan educational programs of several kinds, often with students, other teachers, and members of the community. Such extensions

Personal Domain	Interpersonal Domain	Academic Domain
Trainer, Counselor, Guide	Trainer, Leader, Participant	Trainer, Director, Performer
Training students in personal development; awareness, concentration, meditation, planning, fantasy, improvisation, and invention.	Training in group participation: interpersonal relations, negotiation, co-operation, and leadership.	Training in comprehension, analysis, organization, problem solving, and performance of operations and procedures.
Guiding students in clarifying their own responses, formulating alternatives, making choices, structuring experiences and activities, acting on decisions, and assessing performance.	Leadership and participation in sharing, decision making, formulating plans of action, coordinating effort, resolving difficulties, refining performance.	Directing students through presentations, demonstrations, and organized teaching materials for practice to achieve mastery in content and procedures selected for study. Diagnosis and shared assessment of performance. Assistance in meeting difficulties arising from particular tasks.

have far-reaching implications about the selection, training, and certification of teachers. It will be important for professionals to model an active learning life-style, relate well to others, provide leadership, and possess organizing and planning ability.

An expanded range of learning events and instructional techniques demands an equally expanded range of contexts or environments in which they can occur. The classroom cannot be the world for adolescents; rather, the world should be the classroom. Although only a few of the most distant resources of the global school will be used, and by very few students, there are many environments readily available in the community to supplement textbooks, teachers, and classrooms. Craftsmen, technicians, professionals, libraries, galleries, recreation centers, industrial training units, ruins, rivers and mountains, day-care centers, departments of forestry, and homes can be used. Growth demands contexts of many kinds, stimulating and challenging environments for experience, study, and productive activities. Such resources must be identified, negotiated, and organized to make them available as educational situations. The place for the development of a learning life-style is where the events of life occur.

Program Element 6: To enable students to discover and develop their particular abilities into performative competencies, the range of recognized accomplishment should be greatly extended by providing options within the program, by establishing a field options committee to grant credit for any worthwhile learning experience outside the program, and by establishing an academic options committee to offer more structured learning opportunities within the program. Evaluation can be conducted by measuring each student's accomplishment against a baseline performance in the activity in an appropriate manner.

Conditions for Establishing a Variety of Learning Situations

How can these learning situations be organized to help students create a developmental learning style? Three related conditions seem desirable:

    a. Increase the range of acceptable accomplishment.
    b. Increase the range of options in the ways students may attain those accomplishments.
    c. Evaluate students individually by progress-from-baseline assessment using criteria suitable for the kinds of learning options they choose or are required to take.

One important task of public education is helping students to identify and develop their unique abilities into competencies which provide pleasure and legitimate, not artificially induced, self-esteem. To permit students to enjoy this kind of success, the range of acceptable school accomplishment must include any of the vast array of competencies needed, respected, and beneficial in our society—

all kinds of artistic, technical, organizational, service, research, action-oriented, political, athletic, industrial, professional, as well as purely academic skills. Success in most school subjects depends largely on the basic skills in which students from upper-middle-class homes have a distinct advantage—reading, writing, speaking. These are and should remain important, but readiness to participate in society is not realistically measured by those skills alone. Society needs capable youth, and youth need the confidence that they have abilities the society will recognize.

Holding tight rein on a narrow track is one way of insuring that all students complete at least one kind of high school race. New routes must be opened up so that students can gradually increase their responsibility for choosing their paths. As a consultative educational service rather than directive educational authority, institutions of secondary education can design programs including many student choices and training in how to choose among them. The secondary levels program described in the next section is such a program. But educational institutions, no matter how far-ranging their course offerings, can never identify or organize all possible valuable learning situations. For this reason a field options committee should be empowered to consider any learning experience students propose and to grant credits toward graduation for it. They may include opportunities to travel, work, study independently, pursue an activity, attend institutions out of state or out of the country, or simply to step outside organized programs for a period of time. The field options committee comprises a parent, a school representative, and either a representative involved in the optional activity or another interested adult. They review proposals, meet with the student, negotiate the conditions under which benefits must be demonstrated, and recommend how much credit successful completion of the experience should carry.

Programs that increase the number of options for students are usually offered as alternatives to regular academic schooling. Unless they are separate and fully supported alternative schools in a districtwide system of public schools of choice as described by Mario Fantini, alternative programs tend to operate as troublesome relatives in an otherwise contented academic family. They work often with problem students in ways contradictory to procedures in the regular system. They are frequently marginally supported and tend to be scrutinized with a rigor even the regular school could not withstand. They also tend to leave the familiar form of schooling more undisturbed by siphoning off the disruptive students and nonconformist teachers who might stimulate the regular school's development.

For these reasons, the secondary levels and field options programs are not recommended as alternatives to academic schooling. The secondary levels program is central, but just as the options committee enables students to pursue activities not organized by the system, an academic option enables them to elect coursework more formally structured and directively taught within the system. Student proposals to substitute coursework or other forms of academic study for a limited portion of the regular program will be considered by an academic committee of representatives from the educational system and from the community.

How can progress in such a varied assortment of programs be assessed? In a tight race on a narrow track one simply counts the order as contestants cross the finish line. But what if participants follow various routes to different destinations and few are racing? The problems of assessment involved in a shift from singular to diversified per-

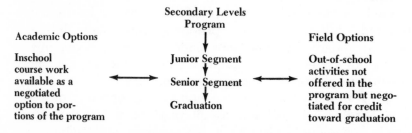

Diagram 7. The Secondary Levels Program in Outline.

formance can be solved, and turned to a distinct advantage, by using a measure appropriate to the activity, and by establishing a baseline performance against which to measure progress. Individuals, student groups, or teachers can plan different programs by proposing a specific improvement in the baseline performance and the criteria by which it will be judged. In consultation, transactions can then be designed to accomplish the desired improvement. (See Diagram 8.) In this way all contestants in the metaphorical track meet of traditional schooling need not be tested by sprinting—or worse, by writing an essay about it—

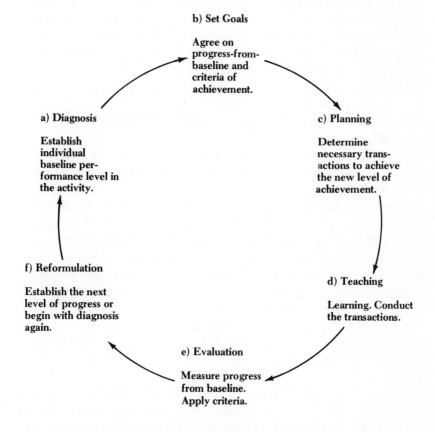

b) Set Goals

Agree on progress-from-baseline and criteria of achievement.

a) Diagnosis

Establish individual baseline performance level in the activity.

c) Planning

Determine necessary transactions to achieve the new level of achievement.

f) Reformulation

Establish the next level of progress or begin with diagnosis again.

d) Teaching

Learning. Conduct the transactions.

e) Evaluation

Measure progress from baseline. Apply criteria.

Diagram 8. The Evaluation of Progress Beyond Individual Baseline Performance.

but by striving for reasonable improvement in an event, whether it is the javelin, pole vault, or the 5000-meter foot race. The key is shifting the emphasis from assessment of knowledge about a field to assessing performance in the field. Knowledge is implicit in the performance but is not sufficient until it is used, whether the area is trigonometry, repairing car engines, leading a group, sculpting stone, writing a newspaper article, playing squash, or serving the community. Improvement in performance is open ended, and assessment is as easily conducted by the student as by others. The progress-from-baseline principle is a useful framework for planning even beyond work in school. Any competitiveness lies primarily with the student and the betterment of past achievement levels. For these reasons, such a system of evaluation is both feasible for secondary education and suitable for a lifelong learning style.

If individuals and small groups of students are working on different kinds of activities toward varying kinds and levels of performance, how can their achievements be recorded and reported?

A student who pursues a series of activities on a learning grid will eventually focus on a particular area of activity and develop a competency ladder. The bottom rung is baseline performance. At various points new levels of performance will be formulated and achieved. The students' record lists those achievements, forming a curriculum vitae of accomplishment. When baseline performance, projected performance, and achieved performance are reported, parents can see not only what has been achieved but what is being attempted and can more easily discuss the students' program and assist in it. The list of performance attainments is a record without prejudice which the student can use in applications for work and higher education.

Breadth of attainment is assured by requiring each student to develop a focus in several learning areas. One framework is outlined in the next section. This is not a *laissez-faire* program. Some activities will be enjoyed for the pleasure they provide. Students will be able to withdraw briefly from the secondary program for breathing space, and within the program they will be able to choose much of what they do and the way in which they will do it. But choose and act they must.

Program Element 7: The secondary program will be divided into two parts: the junior and senior segments. Junior segment students will spend two months in each of eight centers, where they will choose a particular concentration in the areas of art, wilderness adventure and craft, practical investigation procedures, advanced academic studies, humanities and life skills, world study, practical productive skills, and self-directed program development. Senior segment students, with the assistance of their personal committees, will develop challenge programs in seven areas: physical or psychological adventure, creativity, service to others, rational investigation, practical skill, work experience, and academic mastery. In addition, social-recreational programs will be available, community events will be organized, and short-term workshops will be either available or required.

The secondary levels structure must be designed to embody the fourteen propositions for increasing the teaching power of education and the learning power of students. It must define the areas in which learning grids of experiences, studies, and productive activities can be formulated as a basis for personal, group, and directed programs. In secondary levels eight areas of action learning are identified in the junior segment for 13- to 15-year-olds, and eight areas of challenge are identified in the senior segment for 15- to 17-year-olds. Throughout this program students are involved in a core skills program (described in the next section), a social-recreational program, and a program of events organized by members of the community. The elements in secondary levels are outlined in Diagram 9.

Students entering the junior segment from elementary school begin in one of the eight program centers where they remain for approximately two months concentrating on the singular purpose of that center, gradually gaining sufficient range of awareness in the area to choose and pursue a particular in-depth focus. In the Local Bureau of Investigations, for instance, they increase their understanding about the problems encountered in various forms of human activity and the various ways in which people systematically solve those problems. With that increased range of understanding they choose a particular form of investigation, such as the policeman's methods of in-

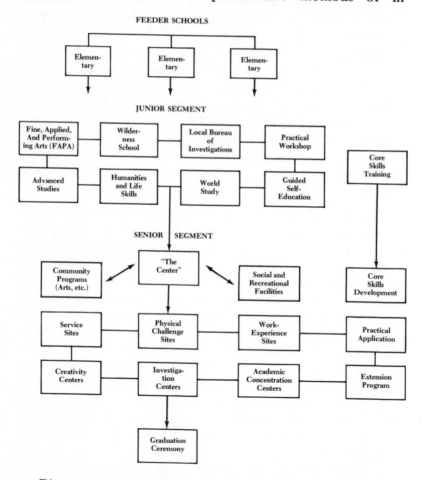

Diagram 9. Outline of Elements in the Secondary Levels Program.

vestigating a crime or the stockbroker's methods of determining what to buy and when to sell, and then design a competency ladder for developing a degree of proficiency in that form of investigation, a proficiency they can demonstrate at the conclusion of the program.

When the two-month period is over, students move to other centers and repeat this process until they have worked in all eight during a period of no more than three years. These eight centers of the junior segment are:

1. The Center for the Fine, Applied, and Performing Arts (FAPA): A wide range of experiences in the ways people express artistic imagination, study in one or more art forms, and progress in one or more forms of artistic expression, such as sculpture, musical instruments, engraving, fashion design, pottery, industrial design, and silversmithing.

2. Wilderness School: Experiencing solitude on solos and individual projects and teamwork in field studies of nature, ecology, and conservation, as well as adventure challenges in the mountains and on the rivers.

3. The Local Bureau of Investigation (LBI): Experiences in a wide range of investigative procedures used by police, chemists, city planners, archaeologists, reporters, and engineers. Study and application of modes of inquiry leading to individual and group investigations.

4. Workshop in Practical Activities: Inventing, designing, making, constructing, repairing, assembling, problem solving in the practical world of machines, electronics, buildings, plumbing, instruments, farming, manufacturing, selling, and city planning. Emphasis is on learning how by doing, leading to individual or group projects.

5. The Institute of Advanced Studies: Intensive academic studies leading to the acquisition of a body of knowledge, concepts, operations, and broad framework of principles in at least two disciplines, and culminating in a presentation and oral examina-

tion by a community committee. Theoretical in emphasis, studies are nevertheless related to concrete experience and practical application.

6. The Humanities Center and Life Skills Laboratory: Focus on personal values and relationships with others through the study of literature, media, and actual behavior; guided self-analysis, role playing, and skill training; and working with community service groups and younger students. Total family participation in the family segment is recommended.

7. Center for the Study of the World: Experience, study, and practice in the dynamics of social, legal, and political processes at local, state, national, and international levels. Learning responsible, active citizenship in the community and the world.

8. School of Guided Self-Education: Students learn to identify interests and abilities, explore alternatives, assemble resources, decide on a focus, set goals, plan a program, confront difficulties, seek appropriate assistance, manage time, and evaluate their own effort and accomplishment. Emphasis is on personal decision making, planning, and performance without the support of a learning-grid structure.

The arbitrary two-month duration may require modification but seems long enough for students to become involved and achieve a level of accomplishment without demanding too extended a period of concentration. Shifting from center to center may be unsettling but is potentially advantageous. It combines uninterrupted concentration with variety and merges opportunities for students to start over again in relationships and performance with a chance to extend the personal, social, and formal skills they have developed. Similarly, it provides teachers time to cultivate demonstrable achievement, and with breaks they have opportunities to assess their programs and plan systematic improvements. Some elements that might be included in a learning grid for developing programs at the Local Bureau of Investigation are listed in Diagram 10 as an example.

	Personal	Interpersonal	Academic
Experience	°Share the experience of someone active in reporting, police-work, or small business operation. °Experience a number of shops, newspapers and precincts as a client and participant. °Experience and record your personal attitudes and responses to the work involved.	°Find out how the adult you are working with feels about hos job, what it means, what he experiences. °Interview people; try selling someone something. °Share your experiences and responses with others.	°Work-study: take over or help with some part of the job. °Experience micro teaching, writing from the wire services, investigating simulated crimes.
Study	°Outline the skills of investigation involved in one of these jobs. °Plan a personal program of study, practice, and activity to master the skills of investigation. Design a competency ladder for developing an important skill involved in the job.	°"Apprentice" to the reporter or teacher learning from them what they do, how, and why. °Establish a base group with others to discuss problems encountered. °Plan an investigation or study of the job with others. °Practice interviewing, selling, teaching others.	°Study technical sources about the work suggested by the teacher or other adult. °Attend the police academy, a night school course in small business management. °Set up classes at the Bureau.
Productive Activity	°Research and write newspaper articles until one is accepted locally for publication. °Prepare and teach a lesson or unit. °Study catalogues, sales, and the market and prepare an order for the business. °Teach others what you have learned.	°Launch a newsletter about the activities of others at the Bureau. °Plan and institute a short-lived small business at the Bureau with others. °Set up a tutoring bureau for younger students.	°Conduct investigations of problems your tutor-model is solving. °Consider other approaches which might be employed and suggest them.

Diagram 10. Some Possible Elements in a Learning Grid for the Local Bureau of Investigation. (Examples are Police Work, Small Business Management, Reporting, and Teaching.)

The junior segment prepares and trains for the greater independence and responsibility of the senior segment. Students begin by meeting with a parent, a teacher, and another adult to begin mapping out challenging programs in the eight designated areas. Students with similar program intentions meet at the appropriate centers where base groups are established for mutual consultation, instruction, and selection of teammates for the two or three challenges which must be conducted in cooperation with others. Learning grids are developed for the exploratory portion of the challenge, and in later meetings with advisors specific achievements are identified and competency ladders for accomplishing them are designed. Some courses will be established to meet emerging needs and others will be required as prerequisites for certain challenges. Students pursuing such activities as scuba diving, mountaineering, or canoeing in the physical challenge, for instance, will be required to take training programs from certified instructors. But generally, students will have free access to sites where they can find the resources, assistance, and guidance they need. The eight challenges in the senior segment are:

1. Physical (Psychological) Challenge: A challenge to the student's daring, endurance, and skill in an unfamiliar environment.

   Examples: Build a kayak and run a river, conduct a solo expedition on the Pacific Crest Trail, learn to climb a 5.5 slope, arrange an exchange with an African student, develop a particular athletic skill to a level of excellence, solo in a light plane, develop a program in meditation or yoga, and so on.

2. Creativity Challenge: A challenge to the student's ability to explore, cultivate, and express his own imagination in some inventive or aesthetically pleasing form.

   Examples: Sculpting, writing poetry, acting, decorative welding, political cartooning, creating Japanese decor and gardens, playing rock music, forming a jazz group or string quartet, performing a stand-up comic's act, cooking gourmet foods, constructing and designing furniture, creating inventions, and so on.

3. Service Challenge: A challenge to identify a human need for assistance and provide what is necessary to fulfill it; to express caring without expectation of reward, preferably through personal interaction with individuals or groups.

Examples: Volunteer work with the young, old, ill, infirm, or retarded; develop such services as a games program for the handicapped, a big brother program for the retarded, trips for shut-ins, activity courses for the aged, crisis work with peers, day-care programs or tutoring for younger children.

4. Investigation Challenge: A challenge to formulate a question or problem of personal importance and to pursue an answer or solution by systematic investigation.

Examples: How does one navigate in space? How much can I control my mind and body through biofeedback? How exactly does a starfish regenerate a lost arm? Can the validity of any psychic experience be proved? What natural, organic means can I use to protect my crops from disease?

5. Practical Skill Challenge: A challenge to explore a utilitarian activity, to learn the knowledge and skills necessary to work in that field, and to produce something of use. This is work one may always do for oneself though perhaps never as a job or profession.

Examples: Write a movie review for a local paper, construct a telescope with hand-ground lenses, develop and manage a section of a farm, create an expert repair service for gas furnaces or electrical appliances, mount a conservation program for an endangered species, design and build a mountain cabin.

6. Work-Experience Challenge: A challenge to work on the job in the community and learn the information, skills, and procedures involved while working closely with a skilled adult or adults.

    Examples: Factories, mills, construction crews, animal hospitals, professional offices, social services offices, newspapers, maintenance crews, local government, private business, artist's studios, stores, and clubs.

7. Academic Challenge: A challenge to organize a coherent program of academic studies—which may include tutoring, laboratory work, and formal courses—in a specific discipline and achieve significant progress beyond baseline performance in it. Whereever possible, academic challenges should be directed toward theoretical understanding of a performative activity.

8. Extension Program: An optional challenge enabling students to pursue one area further, develop a second focus in any challenge area, or create a new challenge which combines areas or establishes a new one.

Students will spend approximately two to three months on each challenge, though individual times will vary, and many may work on two or more simultaneously. Completion of the senior segment within three years will be required. An illustration of the range of elements they may draw upon to develop a program is illustrated in the sample grid for a creativity challenge in wood sculpture outlined in Diagram 11. In addition to the eight challenges, the student is required to continue development beyond baseline performance in the core skills and to participate in several short-term programs which are organized at the center.

At the Center a number of resources, consultants, records,

DEVELOPMENT OF A LEARNING LIFE-STYLE

123

	Individual-Personal	Interpersonal-Social	Impersonal-Academic
Experience	°Learn to experience sculpture in an intense personal way. °Learn to reflect on one's own central images. °Collect sketches, photographs, and samples of compelling objects and shapes. °Develop a personal aesthetics.	°Learn from sculptors and other artists how they feel and think about their work. °Share ideas and experiences or art with peers and others. °Discuss your own work with artists. °Collect wood from mills, lumberyards and orchard owners.	°Find and experience the best sculpture available. °Visit and observe carvers at work. °Visit forestry and wood research laboratories. °Find a work-study job with wood.
Study	°Design a competency ladder in carving. °Learn to visualize vividly. °Carve the same subject many times for skill, precision, and speed. °Plan a personal program of study about the lives, technique, and art of great sculptors. °Plan a program for learning to sketch ideas.	°Apprentice to a master carver. °Plan a program with others to study an art form or historical period of art. °Seek assistance with a carving problem. °Discuss your plans, progress,and problems with a "family" group. °Consult cabinet makers and other specialists.	°Study traditional carving and techniques in books, courses, perhaps in a traditional European school of carving. °Conduct research in selecting, preparing, and drying flitches for carving. °Imitate good carvings. °Practice particular skills, such as sharpening tools, under guidance.
Productive Activity	°Keep a journal of information and a sketchbook of ideas. °Carve and carve and carve. °Create a personal technique and style. °Prepare a show of carvings.	°Teach someone to carve. °Plan a show of various art forms with other artists. °Open a small cooperative shop to sell works of various young artists. °Seek a commission.	°Experiment with new techniques, new equipment, new styles. °Develop new finishes. °Make a file of data on carving woods. °Set up your own studio.

Diagram 11. Some Possible Elements of a Learning Grid for a Creativity Challenge in Wood Sculpture.

and study spaces can also be located. The library may be there along with offices where students can arrange the use of community resources, recreation facilities, workshops and community-sponsored programs. The events arranged by the community program committee include theater performances, speakers, special films, and seminars designed to enrich the range of experiences available in the community and to deal with issues community members consider important. Students will be expected to attend a minimum number but may choose which ones. The recreation committee coordinates all the recreational facilities in the community, arranges for their supervision, and books their use by individuals and groups of students. In addition, the committee arranges—or helps students arrange—a variety of social activities. Workshops, short skill programs necessary for students in dealing with their challenges, may include such activities as human relations training, development of inner-city survival skills, or techniques of organizing community action programs.

These elements of the secondary levels program culminate in a transition ceremony in which students demonstrate their readiness for adult roles in the community.

Program Element 8: Basic skills should be taught in action loops combining skills of experiencing with related process and production skills. They should be taught in direct relationship to ongoing activities. Training in the junior segment should be in how to develop skills in action loops so that the students can independently continue to improve their own performance beyond personal baseline levels in the senior segment.

All educational programs which culminate in the ability to perform an activity must develop skills. The scientific investigator must master research skills; the dress designer, skills for translating drawings into clothes; the kayaker, skills for managing white water. Core skills, which are necessary or valuable in a wide range of activities, are the skills that enable people to learn—to experience, study, and perform—better.

When learning is limited to study in the academic domain then reading, writing, and arithmetic are the basic skills. But when learning also includes experience and productive activity and the personal and social domains, the list of basic skills must be extended. If people do learn by experience, study, and productive activity, then each of these aspects has its own necessary kinds of skills:

Experience	*Study*	*Productive Activity*
Input	Process	Output
Receptive Mode	Integrative Mode	Generative Mode
Perceiving	Thinking	Doing

Further, these elements seem to relate to each other in the form of a cycle, similar to a cybernetic feedback loop, which is outlined in Diagram 12.

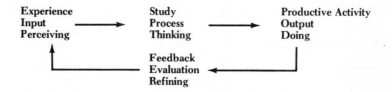

Diagram 12. Skill Training Loop.

This training loop suggests several ways in which skills may be developed effectively. First, it is a basis for identifying skills involved in real life learning and in learning as human development. Second, it suggests a way of relating training in isolated skills to improved performance in important productive activities. Third, it suggests a way of teaching skills so that students can continue to train and improve on their own. When people learn to ski, fly, draw, play a guitar, weld, or build a cabin, they often learn by perceiving what is involved in a good performance, by studying and practicing some part of it, by applying the skill to their own performance, and then by choosing another aspect to improve. Practice of a part is continually integrated with the whole act. In school we too often separate skill training from any real activity, divide clusters of related skills for practice and fail to reassemble them, or reticulate particular skills into minute steps and practice those steps on dull, sometimes demeaning, material. It can be a long way back from isolated skill practice to improved performance in productive activity. Such teacher-directed skill training is also difficult for students to initiate on their own and therefore is of limited value in lifelong learning. Although basic skills are more abstract than such skills as rolling a kayak, they become concrete if directly related to the improvement of performance in valued activities whenever possible.

What are the skills? What are the loops? How will performance be improved? Some of the general skills of functioning are listed in Diagram 13, in relationships which might form skill loops.

Experience Skills	Process Skills	Production Skills
observing	organizing	expressing
manipulating	symbolizing	computing
reading	imagining	applying
*questioning ⟶	analyzing ⟶	problem solving
decision making	planning	acting
feeling	relating	cooperating
self-awareness	conceiving alternative behavior	self-modification
awareness of others	negotiating	leading

Diagram 13. Some Basic Skills of Functioning.

One skill loop could be made from questioning, analyzing, and problem solving. At the Core Skills Center students would learn to solve problems by developing such questioning skills as inquiry strategies and interviewing, such analytical skills as organizing data to discover patterns in it, and such problem-solving techniques as the creative use of analogies and the logical use of scientific method. These skills could be studied while the students were attending the Local Bureau of Investigations so that the skills would have immediate practical application to real problems. In their application of skills to the work of reporters, archaeologists, mechanics, or police officers, students would realize the importance of the skills and discover possibilities for refinement that give direction to further practice. In this manner students would also be learning a method of development, the skill loop, which they could continue to use on their own.

The Core Skills Program in secondary levels attempts to follow the process by which humans develop skill, rather than a logical analysis of the way the skill is performed. The junior segment emphasizes teaching students how to learn in preparation for more self-directed improvement during the senior segment. As in the other elements of secondary levels, students begin by establishing a baseline performance and setting a level of achievement to pursue. Reasonable progress in one's own performance is the only requirement. Consulting with the teacher, the student examines a diagnosis of his performance and plans a practice ladder to achieve his goal. After improving skills needed for the junior segment and learning how to learn those skills, students will be expected to more seriously challenge themselves in these areas and to work on them more independently during the senior segment.

Many methods of mastering these skill loops may be employed, from short-term training seminars and prepared materials to programs planned independently or in small groups. Whatever the method, it must always be designed to improve personal baseline performance and never to cover programs, chapters, or exercises for their own sake. As in sport, the great motivations are the inner satisfaction, recognition by others, and the palpable improvement of performance, which has immediate, important use. Need is the secret of mastery; it leads to dedicated practice in and out of class. Without that practice, an hour or two of training a week isn't likely to change performance very much.

Although this approach to skills is speculative and needs a great deal of further development, it is an extension of the central secondary levels program worth pursuing.

**Program Element 9: The secondary program should cul-
minate in a ceremony which appropriately challenges
students, acknowledges their accomplishment, and
celebrates their moment of transition from school life
to responsible membership in the community. This
could include demonstration of achievement by individual students, a ceremony with family and friends,
and a celebration conducted by members of the community.**

In this model, graduation is a vital, significant part of
the learning process. It culminates the achievement of all
students; it is a time, after all the separate challenges have
been met, of integration during which students present
themselves to their peers, teachers, and community to
demonstrate their achievement of the transformations of
adolescence and their readiness for the social transition
to roles as young adults. It is a celebration of that achievement in some authentic, moving, even ritualistic way.
While familiar markers of this social transition point are
spread over several years—acquisition of a driver's license,
legal adult status, voting rights, noncompulsory school attendance, rights or readiness for marriage—school graduation is the most appropriate time to announce this most
important event, particularly if the school is organized to
prepare students for adulthood. In this program, graduation is a transition ceremony.

The many possible approaches to the ceremony should
be considered in the most inventive ways. High schools
have a tradition of graduation parties which do little more
than celebrate the end of school. They have about as much
relevance to social realities and a learning life-style as a
debutante's ball, and they represent the community's values
about as clearly as a fireworks display. One important
element is a presentation and demonstration by students of
their challenge achievements to an audience of younger
students anticipating their challenges, colleagues who have
shared in some of the challenge work, peers, relatives,
teachers, and other members of the community. Graduates
would demonstrate acquired skills, show filmed records

of their work, display their achievements, and offer oral and written reports outlining their programs. Once introduced, students could make their presentations, interact with their audiences about their work, and receive a formal response to their achievements from representatives of their advisory committees. Many presentations in different rooms throughout the school could go on simultaneously. Brief reports of each challenge, with illustrations, would be filed for entry in the school and public libraries so that others may refer to what has been accomplished and seek the help of those who preceded them, and so that students' accomplishments become part of the Center's recorded history.

The second segment of graduation might be a small dinner in honor of the student—one focusing on relatives, friends, and working colleagues; one emphasizing the closeness of this larger family while announcing the student's formal independence from it. It may include a presentation of the students' aspirations and plans, however tentative, for moving into the next stage of life. It may also include some ritual expressing that closeness and affirming the students' future.

Graduation may conclude with a third segment, a celebration at the school designed to bring students and adults together to celebrate the students' achievements, their formal transition to new roles, and the acceptance of the community welcoming the enrichment they bring to it. This graduation, acting as a goal for students and their helping adults, and as a ritual marker of a major transition in their lives, is fundamentally important to this concept of recurrent education and this model to develop a learning life-style. It represents all periods of transformation and all the transitions in the students' life.

Program Element 10: The participants involved in each center of secondary levels should design and implement their own educational program. A representative council empowered to make program decisions within agreed-upon policy and by agreed-upon procedures should manage centers and other units. Management,

organization, and logistical support should be adapted to the implementation and systematic development of the resulting programs.

Secondary levels introduces major changes in the nature of education and the roles of participants in it which can be successfully implemented only if there are also major changes in the organization and management of education. The most important change will be a reversal in the flow of program decision making from top-down to bottom-up. If students develop personal and group curricula and teachers develop curricula in cooperation with members of the community using a variety of town and country locations to create successful centers, then much planning and decision making usually conducted by executive, state, or district committees and handed down will be made on location and reported up through the organization for approval. Most of the other changes in management will be designed to make this process workable and effective.

In *Free to Learn* John Henry Martin and Charles H. Harrison recommend establishing a large education assembly in each district with elected representatives of each racial and age group charged with the task of guiding the regular improvement of education for all members of the community. Although such proposals are beyond this task force's frame of reference, an educational system capable of promoting lifelong learning and departing from familiar programs clearly requires a broadly representative body with authority to commit a community to greater, more direct involvement in education and to establish organizational patterns and management procedures making involvement workable and productive.

One important task of such a legislative body would be to establish policy and procedures for planning new programs by participants. Perhaps, as indicated in Diagram 14, a program management committee of the assembly could be established for that purpose. By whatever means, guidelines for developing the secondary levels program must guarantee planners the right to consider a broad range of possibilities and, at the same time, must guarantee the community's right to effective and well organized education. This may be accomplished if program development by team members at each center is combined with program review in a secondary levels advisory council of representatives from each unit involved in secondary education.

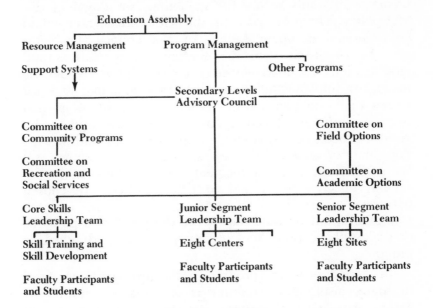

Diagram 14. Organizational Structure for the
Secondary Levels Program.

In the Wilderness School of the junior segment, for example, the overall program would be planned by the teachers and participating adults involved. They would be guided by the charter established in council for that center, by consultation with students and with experts in various fields of wilderness experience, and by established planning procedures. Their work would be facilitated because program participants are more likely to share a common interest, a body of knowledge, and commitment to the purposes of their center than the staff of any regular school. And they will have greater opportunities to improve their program during the breaks between two-month sessions than uninterrupted high school schedules permit. The program plan, once complete, would be presented before the secondary levels advisory council for review. The council, with representation from all the program teams and committees, many of whom must be members of the community, would have full authority to approve and implement programs within the guidelines set down in district policy. The proposal from the wilderness center would be examined in open sessions of the council. Problems may be discussed with the center's representatives and modifications required. Once accepted, plans would be made for implementation, for center evaluation, and for review of the first session of operation. It is important that decisions by the education council be made openly, by known procedures, with wide representation and discussion, and for announced reasons, so that professional and lay participants reach agreements about education in the process of creating it, and so that practices are chosen because they are the most promising for students and the community, not because they serve the political aspirations or philosophical prejudices of any particular individual or group.

In secondary levels, program is the primary imperative. In many institutions program is secondary, compressed within organizational patterns so rigid and management procedures so narrowly defined they dominate it, shape it, and maintain it until little change is possible even when the urgent need for drastic improvement becomes apparent. Unless management procedures are changed to serve open, systematic program development; unless the organizational structure is sufficiently flexible to create new patterns for quite different programs; and unless the logistical support system adapts to the unique needs of unfamiliar educational operations, secondary levels cannot happen, nor can any other major departure from familiar schooling.

While each of these program elements requires a great deal of further refinement and elaboration, they form the building blocks for a model of secondary education designed to cultivate the transformations of adolescence and prepare students for the transition to adulthood, a model in which one major theme is the need for individuals to develop learning life-styles which enable them to grow in fulfillment, understanding, and productivity through all the transitions of their lives.

Given this intention and this model, the question arises, "How can such a program be established when so many circumstances militate against its successful implementation? And if it is established, how can operational problems be eliminated to make it competitive with other programs before it is abandoned?" We now turn to these problems of program development.

CHAPTER VI

New Programs Into
Old Systems Won't Go

Vegetation can survive only in suitable climate and soil; programs can take root and thrive only in a supportive setting. Plant a palm tree in a Pacific Northwest rain forest and it will soon succumb; plant a new program in organizational structures designed to support a familiar high school curriculum and the odds in favor of its survival will be no better. But what kinds of changes are required to create a support system for a program like secondary levels? And how can recommended changes in program and support system be brought about?

Answering these questions involves solving problems in such wide-ranging fields as politics, finance, law, administration, community planning, social interaction, professional training, and instructional methodology, a task beyond the scope of this statement. Yet the issues of support and implementation are crucial. If they are not dealt with, then the new program is no more than a set of blueprints to be stored on the shelf. Basic elements of the support system necessary for secondary levels can be identified; basic problems of implementation and possible solutions can be raised for discussion. That is the purpose of this chapter.

Conversion or Modification?

Support Principle 1: A program of learning events designed primarily to cultivate the transformations and transitions of youth represents a major shift away from familiar secondary schooling rather than an attempt to improve elements of it.

A building can be changed by completely remodeling it for a different purpose or by simply adding a new coat of paint. Similarly, we can change education by redesigning the whole process on a different set of principles or by simply selecting new textbooks. Conversion is a change in the nature of education, its purposes, underlying principles and means. It is the creation of a new model or paradigm. Modification is only an improvement in some aspect of an existing form of schooling.

Secondary levels represents a change in the model of education for adolescents. Emphasis on mastering specific subjects and disciplines is shifted in secondary levels to emphasis on accomplishing the transformations of maturation. Secondary levels guides students into increasingly independent self-directed roles and involves regular studies in real situations, often culminating in challenging tasks in the community. These programs, unlike those in most high schools, are planned by participants. Secondary levels utilizes diverse centers, settings, experiences, studies, and activities and cultivates varied competencies in individuals. While students in regular schools compete against one standard, students in secondary levels compete against their own baseline performances.

The new pattern for secondary education is designed to develop a learning life-style that students will use throughout their lives. It is an open model of community action in which resources and expertise are shared. In these and other ways secondary levels represents a major shift in the education of adolescents toward a pattern in which diverse learning resources are organized for the growth of individuals.

As Thomas Kuhn points out, paradigm conversions occur when the timing is right, when problems, dissatisfac-

tion, and changing circumstances make the old pattern un-
desirable and inappropriate, and when sufficient new
knowledge, theory, and experimental alternative practices
have accumulated to consolidate into a new form. If the
time is not now ripe, a shift—from a directive, terminal,
production model for achieving specific objectives in academic studies in school to a diverse, lifelong ecological
model for achieving the potentials of growth in all aspects
of human development through the full resources of the
community—seems to be appearing. If the time has come
for secondary levels or another form which effectively
translates the emerging model into an operating system, it
will still need a vehicle by which it can arrive.

**Support Principle 2: The nature of the school system con-
trols the nature of learning events in the school program. To change the nature of learning events requires
an equal and appropriate change in the school system,
which necessitates a change in the system of supporting structures.**

Content is shaped by its context; the school program is
controlled by the system which is its context. Creating a
new program without creating a new system appropriate to
it guarantees that the new program will be very much like
the old one—or that where the new program conflicts with
the old system it will be neutralized by resistance or made
inoperable by the lack of supportive structures. When new
programs and the systems in which they function are conceived together, two important advantages can be realized:
the system may support the program and cultivate its success, and the system may add its powerful influences on
learning to the messages of the program. To maximize
these benefits, structure should be designed in an inter-
dependent relationship with program content. Then structure may be changed to influence learning and suggest developments in program as readily as program developments
may suggest or require new structures.

School innovations often require little change in the
support system, perhaps because it predetermines most of

the significant elements which might be changed. A grade
10 English course, for instance, may be changed by selecting new novels and regularly forming small groups to discuss questions suggested in a new curriculum guide, but
the course will still be in a grade organization, in a subject
called English, for the discussion of questions about novels
from a curriculum guide in a classroom. The course may be
an excellent one, but not because of the changes, for most
of the elements which influence behavior will not have
been changed at all.

A more radical program change introduced within an
old structure raises havoc; it makes demands the operating system is not designed to meet, it interferes with complex interactions developed in the support system, and it
requires the invention and integration of new operations
to meet the new demands. Consider the problems for the
innovator and for the system when a regular high school
introduces a week-long program of residential outdoor education. It introduces new roles and methods, creates new
liabilities, withdraws students from other subjects, alters
the pattern of supervision and evaluation, and separates
one group of students and faculty from others. In addition,
the new program requires special permissions, special
supplies and transportation, a special location, unique program materials, special financing, and some means of
covering new risks. A system long established to maintain
the familiar program will resist this interference and these
demands. The new program cannot function without the
necessary support system. If the innovator must negotiate
all the necessary administrative arrangements, a combina-
tion of resistance and exhaustion will likely soon terminate
it.

Godwin Watson, in *The Planning of Change*, quotes
Sorenson and Dimock's finding: "No part of institutional
change is an 'island unto itself': Changes in program call
for changes in every other part of the institution . . . and
advance in one sector cannot proceed far ahead of change
in other sectors." Nor is setting up an alternative structure
within the system a promising solution because, he argues,

"The sad fate of experimental schools . . . indicates the power of the larger system to impose its norms even on units which have been set apart, for a time, to operate by different standards and expectations." Over time, organizational patterns and norms increase their domination of the program until familiar structures are regarded as necessary and maintaining the organization becomes an unquestionable virtue.

Yet in a developing system, organization is adapted to serve program formulation, implementation, and management. In growth the two are interactive. To function successfully, the secondary levels program outlined in Chapter 5 requires an appropriate support system far different from existing ones. Because it is a major change in program, it requires a major change in the organization within which it operates so that program and organization form a coherent system.

Support Principle 3: Changing the support structure for a program involves appropriately changing the planning and decision-making process; the arrangement of organizational patterns; the legal, political, and financial conditions governing its operations; the environments of the program; the roles and relationships of participants; and the methods and materials of learning and teaching.

The model for a program support structure includes these elements in this order. Each element represents a major influence on the program by determining whether the learning events will occur, how easy it will be to conduct them in the desired way, and how successfully their goals will be achieved. Each element also influences the others. The order sought in the design of this model is from most pervasive effect to least pervasive effect, from the element with the greatest control over the others to one with least control. (See Diagram 15.) If this can be done accurately, a list is turned into a guide for designing a support system in which all the elements are coherent with the program and with each other. When a support structure for secondary levels is designed according to this model, each element of the familiar school structure is changed:

1. Process. Introducing a process in which each center plans its program within a system of formal approval and review and in which the teacher's responsibilities to implement are matched with the administrator's responsibilities to support.
2. Organizational Patterns. Creating organizational patterns that establish working relationships with necessary community and regional organizations, so

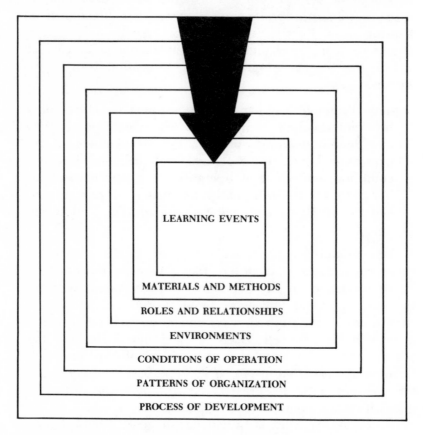

LEARNING EVENTS

MATERIALS AND METHODS

ROLES AND RELATIONSHIPS

ENVIRONMENTS

CONDITIONS OF OPERATION

PATTERNS OF ORGANIZATION

PROCESS OF DEVELOPMENT

Diagram 15. Dimensions of a Setting for the Development of Educational Programs.

that the resources necessary for learning are co-ordinated and available for use; and in which teachers, students, and others are brought together for planning and implementing the program.

3. Conditions. Negotiating conditions which make it legally possible, operationally convenient, and professionally desirable for all parties involved to participate in the process of development.

4. Environments. Identifying the broadest possible range of environments to select the most appropriate context for particular learning experiences.

5. Roles and Relationships. Developing new roles in which the community and school share responsibility for creating educational events and the student is more clearly responsible for learning; developing relationships with more open and sustained communication and more equal status among all participants.

6. Materials and Methods. Selecting and developing materials and methods by participants according to the students' needs for growth in the personal, social, and academic domains of experience, study, and productive activity.

These elements of the support system sustain the operation of the program.

7. Learning Events. Planning experiences of students intended to accomplish the purposes of the program—in this case, the program of events in the junior and senior segments of secondary levels.

These elements not only enable secondary levels to occur, but also influence the resulting learning. The effect of the support structure depends on the coherence of the elements with each other and with the program.

Support Principle 4: Major program change requires a change in the planning and decision-making process. In secondary levels this means changing to a systematic development of programs by professional and com-

munity participants and operating within policy guidelines established by a broadly representative assembly
and appointed committees. Programs will be presented
for approval through an advocacy procedure; development will be monitored by regular external program
review.

Authority in planning is authority to control the nature of all the other elements in the support structure.
Decisions governing the nature of school programs now
flow from the state political authority to teachers and students in classrooms. A shift in program requires redis-
tributing the rights and responsibilities in decision making and establishing a new pattern of implementation.
Secondary levels does not require reversing the present
pattern—making teachers completely autonomous in determining what they teach or students independent in choosing what they study—but it does require assigning them
major responsibility for developing a program and constructive means for higher authorities to monitor the quality
and improvement of each program in the system.

From one perspective, secondary levels is a structure
for program planning, decision making, and action. Because one purpose of the system is to graduate students
with a learning life-style, they plan a portion of their activities from the time they begin attending. Each center
is designed to enable teachers with shared interests and
skills to coordinate community resources, student activities,
and their own instruction into a program to develop one
kind of competence. The secondary levels advisory committee maintains coherence among the various centers
and a high standard of performance through procedures
for the approval and regular review of all programs. So
that for major changes community members as well as professionals are represented, the secondary levels program—
like all other educational programs in the district—is governed by a large, broadly based education assembly. And
to insure the rights and responsibilities of all participants
in planning and implementing, the assembly will supervise

the composition of a district educational constitution. In these ways the support system can insure participation, facilitate implementation, and monitor the quality of the district's programs.

The school, as John Goodlad states, is the appropriate organic unit for educational planning and change. At each center of secondary levels students, teachers, and adults are grouped in several ways for planning and learning in a variety of related locations. Formulating and coordinating activities in each of the sixteen centers can be conducted most effectively by their participants. If teachers and other adults with little training in any formal procedure must plan, however, the process which occurs in each secondary levels center must also be guided by the structure. This can be accomplished by adopting a general vision of what education could become, a systematic planning process, a means of outside approval, a procedure for regular review and assessment, and a regular relationship with experts.

Conversion begins with a shared vision of education in the new model. Without a vision, statements of specific behavioral goals and objectives are often merely precise descriptions of what one has been attempting. With a vision, goals become statements of aspiration, descriptions of what is not yet but will be pursued. Vision is as practical a necessity to the developer as a compass to an explorer; without one he travels aimlessly, lacking priorities to guide choices and action. In this instance, the vision proposed for all participants is specifically the secondary levels program. Each center should also begin by formulating a vision so that the center's intentions can be communicated to others. Each district's vision may be different, but it will be a bond necessary for coherent progress in planning.

The procedure for systematic program development outlined in the discussion of proposition 12 in Chapter 3 is one way various centers can use planning as a continual search for improvement in education and as continued progress toward realization of the vision. It begins with identifying teaching-learning problems to be overcome or opportunities to be pursued and agreeing on priorities for

action. In the second stage all the alternatives are explored
and an improved model incorporating the desired improvements is creatively formulated. In the third stage, while
the model is used in the field, its effects are monitored
and regular changes refine it. The final stage may be formal research to evaluate the approach, dissemination of
the program, if it is successful, or return to the identification and formulation stages of the process.

Effectiveness may be increased, as Seymour B. Sarason
suggests, by delaying decisions until the universe of alternatives has been explored, rather than assuming that
choice is narrow or dictated by familiar circumstances.
Ronald G. Havelock also recommends gathering a large
sample of the resources available for the program and for
planning it so that better choices of materials and methods
can be made. Planning effectiveness can also be increased
by using some strategies for formulating conceptual
models, perhaps the metaphor and analogy technique
recommended for problem-solving groups by William J. J.
Gordon, or lateral thinking as recommended by Edward
de Bono. Participation by untrained members of the community will become effective more swiftly if a step-by-step
process for developing educational programs is developed;
based, perhaps on the schema designed by Alexander,
Ishikawa, and Silverstein for citizen participation in planning multipurpose community buildings. Each planning decision is formulated as a problem, alternatives are outlined,
the known results of each choice are detailed, and a discussion of the problem is published in separate pamphlets.
The pamphlets comprise a reference book which can be expanded, weeded out, or changed as developments dictate.
In these ways, seldom used in education, programs can be
better planned, implemented, and refined.

A procedure for examining and approving program proposals can insure quality and coordinate programs throughout the district. A procedure for review and assessment
can monitor performance and guide improvement. Open
discussion leading to rational decisions is more likely to
occur when program approval results from advocacy pro-

ceedings. This use of informal courtroom procedures in programming, explored by Tom Owens and others at the Northwest Regional Educational Laboratory in Portland, can insure a balanced examination and ruling. When a junior segment center presents its program plan to the secondary levels advisory council, for example, the proposal is circulated in advance. The adjudicating committee, perhaps the council itself, officiates at the hearing. One advocate represents the affirmative, another the negative; one attempts to illuminate the program's strengths, the other its weaknesses. With a minimum of courtroom convention, the discussion can be pointed and constructive, and the emphasis on evidence and reasoning can be maintained. Being public and open, the deliberations can communicate the nature of the program as well as reach a decision that avoids both back-room manipulation and general indifference. More important, such approval hearings communicate the nature of programs to representatives of other centers who attend. Similarly, renewing approved programs and maintaining the developmental process can be achieved by regular, extensive review of each center by examiners appointed by the center and by the advisory council. The purpose of these regular reviews, like the approval hearing, is to maintain vigilance over the programs, but more important, to keep the proper questions before participants, provide constructive recommendations for program improvement, confirm the center's achievements, and reaffirm the shared rights and responsibilities of the whole community for each part of the program. Conducted in this spirit, it is an energizing as well as constructive and necessary part of the process of program development.

Finally, the structure can contribute to planning in each center by making a team of consultants available. The consultant is an advisor, serving the needs of the center rather than any personal academic or research needs. And it is a long-term commitment arranged, perhaps, through a university which accepts school service as partial fulfillment of professorial responsibilities.

The secondary levels advisory council is appointed by the district educational assembly,* the governing body of all local educational services. Larger than present school boards, it is broadly representative of education and the community. If the school is the appropriate organic unit for planning programs, such an assembly seems to be the appropriate organic unit for determining district policy, appointing supervisory committees, and approving major changes in program as well as the changes in organization they will demand. State authorities cannot make decisions suitable for widely divergent districts. Local authorities cannot be expected, legally, to redistribute their power or responsibilities. Teachers, students, and other members of the community may employ political or legal mechanisms but otherwise lack any process for ongoing influence on the shape and nature of the program and the system. The assembly combines a locus and procedure for the district educational debate, carries the authority to act on decisions, and balances the right of the community to participate with its responsibility to contribute.

But techniques for planning and routes for decision making still require a statement of principles to guide and insure their proper use. This statement, the key document in the creation of a setting for program and system renewal, is the district educational constitution. It describes the roles of all participants, assures their rights and responsibilities, and outlines the processes by which they function. The important point is that the constitution guarantees that decisions properly planned and approved will be implemented and supported.

Development, especially on the scale suggested in this model, requires open discussion, which depends upon the certainty of one's right to speak without threat. Discussion in planning is fruitless if it does not lead to decision and action. Participants cannot speak freely if that right is not guaranteed; discussion will not necessarily lead

*Arguments for such an assembly are presented by John Henry Martin and Charles H. Harrison.

to decisions unless procedures are clearly prescribed; and decision will not be implemented unless the responsibilities as well as the rights of all participants to act on decisions are binding. As the statement of these rights, responsibilities, and procedures, the constitution is debated, agreed upon, and confirmed by all the participants. As such it may be the basic instrument for creating a setting in which a major shift can occur and programs such as secondary levels can be conceived and prosper. If schools and districts do not now have such constitutions, democracies such as the United States have excellent models of their formulation and use.

In these ways, a coherent system of planning can be designed to support the creation of secondary levels programs and the other elements of the support structure.

Support Principle 5: Major program change requires new organizational patterns. Secondary levels is based on three patterns of organization: learning grids leading to competency ladders; differentiated centers in the junior and senior segments; and program management groups led by the education assembly, the program committee, and the secondary levels advisory committee. In addition, a pattern must be developed to organize diverse educational agencies and community groups on whose cooperation and resources the program depends. And a pattern for flexible logistical support must be developed so that the diverse and changing needs of various centers can be met.

Patterns of Organization in the Delivery System

The patterns of organization for center programs and for program management in secondary levels are described in Chapter 5. Briefly, they involve the following:

1. Programs in each center will be developed from learning grids of experiences, studies, and activities in the personal, social, and academic domains; they will lead to individual and small group programs

based on competency ladders and skill loops designed to improve baseline performance.

2. Secondary levels will consist basically of a junior
segment involving eight differentiated centers and a
skill training center and a senior segment of eight
challenge sites, a skill development center, field and
academic options, community-organized programs,
and social-recreational activities.

3. Program management will begin with the formation
of an education assembly and a district education
constitution. A program committee will be appointed to establish, monitor, and manage programs
for the whole community. The program committee
will formulate program policy to govern the secondary levels advisory council. In each center, individuals and groups will consult with their committees
for program approval and review; center staff will
present their programs to an adjudicating committee
in open session of the advisory council and will review their program each year with a consulting team.

Two other patterns of organization are also necessary:
one to organize community resources required in the program, and one to organize agencies with direct influence
on the program.

As Edwin P. Rubens concludes in *Planning for Children
and Youth Within National Development Planning,* many
resources and organizations for the welfare, guidance, and
education of youth exist. They are sufficient in most countries, states, and municipalities to support a wide range of
improved programs. But these resources lie fallow because
they are scattered through many different sectors of the
economy. He argues that these resources can and should
be coordinated by a committee representing all agencies
dealing with youth directly or indirectly. Through such a
committee separate agencies could negotiate a priority for
contribution to the education of youth and then could organize an integrated resource for such new community-
based programs as secondary levels.

Rubens is concerned with a national consultative

committee for the strategic and maximum use of resources for care and education of the young. If pilot studies of programs based on the secondary levels model should lead to widespread use, such a committee at the highest level would seem necessary. Even during pilot studies, however, regional and local committees with a similar membership and purpose are necessary elements of secondary levels. The task of mobilizing such committees is complex, requiring the identification of appropriate agencies and representatives, organizing them into appropriate bodies, choosing incentives and operating procedures, and developing a working system of operations through which the services represented can be used. The people involved will have to be influential in their fields and have decision-making power to modify the operation of their agencies. In a change of this magnitude, reaching into almost every sector of the community, the object is not to seek help from a better home and school organization or PTA but to organize the community as school.

A regional committee should be established—representing such central educational agencies as district authorities (e.g., education assemblies), teacher training institutions, state agencies for schools and colleges, and an independent schools alliance—to negotiate suitable regulations, funding, teacher education and reeducation, and facility sharing. District committees will be required to negotiate the use of diverse services and to integrate them into a readily available educational resource. They seem to fall into four main groups, which may be represented more appropriately as separate committees rather than one:

1. Peripheral educational agencies: private vocational training schools, government vocational training programs, on-the-job training centers, night school programs, institutions for training in specific areas such as dance and human relation skills, Boy Scouts, Outward Bound, the YMCA and YWCA, hobby and interest groups, and so on.
2. Community organizations: federal, state, and local

governments, religious and private agencies involved in delivering services in health, education, social, recreational, and cultural fields.

3. Business and industry: all forms of business, primary and secondary industry, the professions, the professional arts and crafts, competitive services, and labor organizations.

4. Unobtrusive enterprises: the completely nonorganized legions of experts and specialists who work alone, after closing time, at home, and often without profit: cabinet workers, inventors, artists, designers, chefs, boat builders, and so on. These include the many retired but active experts in every field.

These are the four main areas which must be organized through a central group in the district to make available the resources necessary for secondary levels. Community service groups such as the Rotarians may agree to coordinate the resources of business and industry. Most districts have a community information center which can identify the services available. The cooperation of the media may be enlisted to reach individuals working at unobtrusive enterprises. But these represent the barest beginnings in a challenging organizational task.

Finally, a central brokerage service must be established in the district with complete records on the resources available, procedures for matching up individuals and groups with the desired resource, and a means of guiding and monitoring the quality of both experience and performance. Ivan Illich, in discussing the concept of learning webs, suggests three other ways the student can "gain access to any educational resource which may help him to define and achieve his own goals" besides a directory of educators-at-large: 1) a reference service to educational objects which would be reserved for student use in institutions such as libraries and laboratories or available to use at locations such as factories and farms; 2) a skill exchange in which students and others list the skills they are able and willing to model for those who wish to learn them; and 3) a peer-matching communications network for students to establish partnerships in pursuit of shared interests and curiosities.

These organizational patterns at the national, regional, and local levels indicate the kinds of enabling and cultivating conditions which must be established.

Support Principle 6: Major program change requires change in the conditions of the system. Secondary levels will more likely occur if cultivating conditions such as time, rewards, special training, support, and resources are focused on program development; and if enabling conditions reduce the liability of school personnel, modify hiring policies and college entrance requirements, modify union policies enabling youth to work and adults to teach, adopt new teacher training practices, and perhaps change compulsory education requirements. Secondary levels also requires legislation to make the program legal, the cooperation of business and industry advantageous, and systematic development and review mandatory.

Consider the conditions which had to be created to insure that all children would be protected from abusive work and sent to school for ten to twelve years for an academic education. The complexities were staggering: a population to convince, laws to pass, a curriculum to create, teachers to be trained, buildings and books to be supplied, state and local agencies to be organized, and regulations to be passed to govern the new system. Changing conditions to make possible secondary levels, or any program like it, is no less complex. Three kinds of necessary conditions will be briefly discussed: cultivating conditions to encourage participants to commit themselves to the program; enabling conditions to make it possible for the program to occur; and requirements which must be set down to insure the legality of the program.

Bringing people together to decide on education, the constitution, the development process, and the organizational patterns are all essential conditions for implementing secondary levels. More generally, such conditions as the following will tend to cultivate education in the new mode:

1. Time: Time is a scarce commodity in most educational planning, but without lead time for useful preparation or time off from other duties, little planning of depth or significance is likely.
2. Reward: All the rewards of the organization must be tied to the kind of behavior it seeks. The school system announces what behavior it seeks by rewarding it with promotions, recognition, choice opportunities, or increased freedom of action. Participants in the system read this message very clearly. It should say "Develop!"
3. Support: Those who decide and implement new programs must act on behalf of the organization and be confident of support in their efforts, even when problems arise.
4. Resources: New programs usually require new resources, equipment, materials, personnel, transportation, and so on. School officials must be committed to making necessary resources available, unless drastic unexpected inequities in cost-benefits arise.

The most crucial conditions will be those which enable the gears of secondary levels to mesh with the machinery of the community. They include:

1. Liability: Many teachers, schools, and districts are too frightened of liability and court action if any student or teacher is injured or suffers as a result of activities endorsed by the school. Such an attitude seriously represses the development of programs which occur off campus under conditions making supervision difficult. Yet all parties have a right to reasonable protection. Conditions must be established in which responsibility is shared by all participants and school and faculty members are appropriately insured.
2. Hiring policy: When students seek jobs, the employer

usually requests their records and recommendations from the school. When the school provides such information it invades the student's privacy and may place itself in an adversary position. It may also unjustly condemn the student who did poorly and caused trouble in school but is perfectly capable of doing the job and has changed completely from the person described in his records. Such punishment for shortcomings or "crimes" in school and punishment after finishing school is unjust. Hiring policy based upon the amount of schooling is also an unjust practice when additional schooling has nothing to do with increased ability to do the job. Further, students in secondary levels will not have a record of grades in the usual academic courses but may be skilled and qualified. For this reason, employers must agree to develop a method of screening applicants solely on their ability to do the job advertised.

3. University entry: For similar reasons, universities and other institutions must find ways to screen students according to their capacity to benefit from higher education, rather than their academic histories as recorded by others. James Bellanca and Howard Kirschenbaum reported in 1973 that the majority of colleges already admit high school graduates without reference to grades or class rank.

4. Teachers unions: Teachers unions and certifying agencies must be approached to create a much broader definition of who can teach, where, and when.

5. Teacher education: Alternatives to present training practices must be sought to find ways of preparing teachers for program planning, organizing community resources, and guiding, as well as instructing, students. The possibility of a school district training teachers for a secondary levels program should be considered, and possibilities of securing certification for them—and for adult participants with qualifications but not the training—should be explored.

6. Compulsory education regulations: Pilot studies should be conducted to determine whether lowering the age of compulsory education encourages students to seek alternatives and schools to develop them.
7. Labor unions: Labor unions must be approached to create a category of students clearly defined as workers-in-training at a lower minimum wage and to become actively involved in programs for education of youth.
8. Child-labor laws: Child-labor laws should be reviewed to extend the range of jobs student workers-in-training may legally perform. At present even 16- and 17-year-olds are excluded in some states from such activities as operating a metal lathe in a commercial machine shop.

In addition to these cultivating and enabling conditions, without basic requirements the program will be immobilized. Two important requirements are the development of a suitable logistical support system and the enactment of necessary legislation. Designing a support system to provide such essentials as financing, new environments, equipment, supplies, transportation, districtwide communication, and so on places a new and different task before management. The challenge of secondary levels, and the districtwide education for citizens of all ages it implies, is the development of a logistical system meeting new demands for the purchase, supply, and support, for instance, of a wilderness center or a district educational communication network. This means developing new patterns; it also means developing a flexible process of problem solving to meet the regularly changing needs of a system which is itself continually developing improved approaches. The excellence of a professional office staff will be its ability to make improvement feasible rather than to make the familiar unavoidable.

Another required condition is that legislation be passed to make a secondary levels system legal; to make cooperation by business, industry, and other institutions financially advantageous or required by law; and to make systematic development mandatory. Before a program like secondary levels can occur, many state laws and regulations governing such aspects as the requirements for high school graduation or for specific curriculum content will have to be drastically changed. If the cooperation of business and industry is to be sustained and energetic, rather than token public relations, tax benefits or some other advantages must be available for participants. On such legal and financial grounds, quality experience and training can be negotiated and regulated. Finally, the underlying argument in this Platform Statement is that systematic program development should be a professional way of life; secondary levels based on the propositions cited encourages such growth. While it would be improper to suggest that secondary levels be legislated, it is appropriate to recommend that some form of systematic development be required by law so that authorities are both permitted and expected to propose and pursue ambitious improvements in the education of adolescents.

The planning process, organizational patterns, and operating conditions established in law and practice will influence the nature of the physical environments and the cultural setting of interpersonal interactions which develop.

Support Principle 7: Major program change requires the development of physical environments which enable the program to occur and which contribute their effects to the intended learning. Secondary levels requires out-of-school locales of different kinds. Many of the sixteen centers will be unique, and all may employ diverse subsidiary locations. If some centers—such as a center for fine, applied, and performing arts—are designed for intensive, multiple use by people of all ages and abilities, several purposes of the program will be served.

Environment is a major influence on the maturing process. The circumstances of the individual's life at home, in the community, at school, and in the world influence behavior and growth. They limit the opportunities for development, determine the degree to which people's potential for development is realized, and shape the kind of persons they will be—their physical stature, health, intelligence, perception, personality, attitudes, and work and behavior patterns. In this process, the general circumstances seem more important than the details. In fact, behavioral psychologists argue that this backdrop can be staged to determine the kind of behavior that will occur on it. In education we are traditionally more concerned with the curriculum of messages than the conditions under which they are communicated. But if we are attempting to have a significant impact on student learning, the environmental medium must be congruent with messages the system wishes to convey to students, which are in this case to grow and mature—become self-directing, responsible, caring, and competent. In this section some aspects of the physical-structural environment will be introduced, and in the next, the human-social environment will be discussed, although the two are interactive and difficult to separate.

What environments are congruent with the proposed learning activities of secondary levels? In Chapter 3 the proposition of the community as school and school as a community resource was stated; in Chapter 5 the various centers and sites required for secondary levels were outlined; in this chapter the problems of identifying and organizing the array of resources available and necessary were discussed. These provide a general answer to the question of environments for the transformations, negotiations, and transitions of youth. It is important, however, to emphasize some aspects of environments which not only provide a place where the program can happen but also clearly reflect the program's messages. To utilize suitable environments for experience, study, and activity in the personal, social, and academic domains at any center, locations which have seldom been required for schooling before must be identified. Consider the settings necessary even for the few examples in Diagram 16.

To be congruent with the developmental nature of the program, two principles—increasing range and depth—be-

	Personal	Social	Academic
Experience	solitude	mountain climbing with a team	attending the theater
Study	a bio-feed-back program	immersion in the French language	on-site study veterinary practice
Productive Activity	carving wood sculpture	a team project in care of the elderly	developing a computer program

Diagram 16. Examples of Learning Activities
Demanding a Wide Range of Environments.

sides the adaptation of setting to function should guide the selection of diverse locales and the order in which students experience them. The principle of increasing range is that adolescents require an arena of experience, study, and productive activity expanding through various kinds of locales—nature, industry, social service center, theater, and studio, for instance—and through various degrees of extension beyond the familiar harbors of home, neighborhood, and school to the community, the nation, and the world. The principle of increasing depth is that adolescents require an increasing depth of involvement in any particular locale, from observation of an activity to participation and greater responsibility to function maturely in it.

Although it will always be impossible to find all the locations needed or even ideal examples of each kind, the range of environments vastly increases once the mind-set about school as a particular edifice is broken. Public institutions such as museums, galleries, parks, zoos, courts, libraries, and recreation centers are already available. Locations in business, industry community services, educational institutions, and other centers of adult activity can be negotiated. The potential of the home as a learning center with media, equipment, communications systems, recreation space, and other resources can be more effectively developed and utilized. Many of the centers requiring such resources can be located in school buildings. But new kinds of centers will be required—for fine, applied, and performing arts and for wilderness activities, for example—and if these are to be established with a high cost-benefit ratio they should be designed for intense use. This can be accomplished by designing them for multiple use, for use by younger students and adults as well as adolescents, and by designing them to be used in a variety of ways. For example, the Center for Fine, Applied, and Performing Arts could be a resource center where people can explore the arts, practice on individual projects without taking a course, find informal and formal training at various levels, and where professionals in performance and preparation can mingle with amateurs and the casually interested. Such a center where adolescents can learn from adults and teach the young would be a model environment for secondary levels and for a community designed to cultivate a learning life-style among all its citizens. It is a practical example of how environments can be conceived so that they facilitate solving such problems as staffing as well as making desirable activities possible and reflecting the message of the program.

John Goodlad speaks of school as a concept rather than a place. A concept of a learning society in which individuals develop throughout their lives carries education beyond the school to the community, to the society as a whole, and to the world at large. Ultimately, the world is the environment for learning and the world population is the learning society in which each individual shares the urgent developmental tasks of communication, understanding, and cooperation. Isolation is no longer a realistic or hopeful alternative. The media, travel, political and economic interdependence, and the common threat of annihilation bind all people and countries together in a shared life and mutual destiny. The concept of education embodied in this work is a small move toward that program in that environment.

Support Principle 8: Major program development involves a major change in the roles and relationships of all participants. In secondary levels, teachers will be ac-

tive in a broader range of professional activities: planning and organizing learning situations in the school and community and fulfilling a variety of instructional roles. Students will have an increasing responsibility for designing their own learning and pursuing new kinds of activities. Parents and other adults will be more directly involved in the school centers and in working with students. In fulfilling these roles, new purposes and new groupings for different kinds of operations will create new patterns of interaction among the participants. Training, support, protective assurances, and other means of assisting them in their new roles and relationships will be essential.

The greatest influence of an educational environment is likely generated by the people in it, the roles they fulfill, the relationships among them, and the ongoing relationship they establish with the student. The social environment and the socialization of students it stimulates—for better or for worse—will have a major influence on student learning no matter what the content and skills being dealt with. If the principles of cooperation are taught in an autocratic social setting, for example, students may learn to verbalize the principles but may be even less likely to practice them than before. A human environment congruent with the purposes of secondary levels is critical for its implementation.

In creating such an environment, the most profound change will be in the new roles and relationships of all participants. Among them, the teacher will experience the most profound and demanding change. The role will involve less presentation of content and more organization of people, resources, and events to create learning situations for students. Teachers will plan what is presented rather than present what is planned by others. While they may still direct students, their success will be measured by the swiftness with which students learn, as a result of teaching, to direct their own programs independently and with others. And while knowledge of academic content will be necessary, it will no longer be sufficient in most roles. Familiarity with the source of theory and the ability to apply knowledge in productive activity will be equally important. Like students, teachers will no longer be isolated from the community; they will spend more time organizing, working with, guiding, and training adults in various circumstances. Changes in their role will be matched by changes in their relationships with others. At different times they will be consultants, guides, leaders, instructors, and planners. And in training for this new role, the most important feature will be the development of a professional learning life-style so that teachers who develop programs are themselves always developing as professionals. Modeling such a life-style for students may be the most important teaching they do.

The role of students in this scheme is also radically changed. While they will experience greater freedom of choice and movement, they will also shoulder increasing responsibility for learning as the program progresses. Learning—maturing, developing self-awareness, becoming competent, mastering teamwork, planning programs, assuming adult roles, contributing to others, formulating a learning life-style—will be the adolescents' work. By promoting responsible pursuit of that work, education can cultivate their commitment to their own becoming and may tap the deepest reservoirs of motivation. The role of the student is learning to seek an education. Parents fulfill an important role in this process. By understanding and valuing their children's development, they will more likely encourage it. By taking part in many of the decisions, they will learn more quickly what is involved in adolescent development and be better able to contribute to it. By creating an arena for parent-school and parent-child participation, education in this mode fosters dialogue, gives it focus, and enables community members to take an important part in the school's activities. As a result, parents may be more likely to contribute their time and expertise to secondary levels programs as well as to their children's other activities. Parents and other members of the community not only will be important elements of the program but also will take part in planning through the centers, committees, and the advisory council. In other words, they will become directly involved in all levels of the educational system. Becoming part of the interpenetration of school and community not only will bridge the separation of the two but also will match new rights to participate in school decisions with new responsibilities to assist in their implementation. The role of professional staffs in developing program support systems, the role of teacher training institutions in preparing teachers for their new functions, and the role of researchers and other academicians in becoming actively involved as problem-solving consultants for the emerging system are summarized in Appendix III.

In fulfilling these roles, participants will establish patterns with social interactions occuring more often, more intensely, and with a greater range of other people than is common in familiar schooling. Through such interactions, individuals from the school and the community will become cooperative groups, and programs will be planned and implemented. Through these relationships, students can accomplish much of their learning from peers, adults in the various centers, or adults in the community. It is important, therefore, that these individuals and their relationships with each other model behavior worthy of emulation by students, and that their relationship with students cultivate their maturity and prepare them for adulthood rather than prolong their dependence, inexperience, and incompetence.

In light of the nature and intensity of these important interactions, it is also important to organize the social setting for what Sarason calls "ongoing programmatic regularities" within the one system which are satisfying and productive for all participants. In such major social change, not only the effectiveness but also the very survival of the program depend on the willingness of the people involved to maintain it. This means that the culture of the institution—the patterns of interaction established over time—must be as improved for the participants as the program of learning or neither will endure. A more authoritative analysis and field development of a cultural setting to sustain new modes of behavior are required, but some aspects can be cited:

1. Planning teams to design individual and various center programs bring people together with a suitable structure for accomplishing their task.
2. Shared decision making, responsibility, and outside review encourage cooperation.
3. A common focus among participants in each center and guiding procedures for their various operations will give their cooperation direction and a process for accomplishment.
4. Supplying resources, time, guarantees of outside support, consultation with experts, and inservice training will encourage personal and professional growth among participants and the fulfillment of their roles.
5. Increased visibility in the community combined with increased cooperation from the community will balance any new anxiety with support.

Such elements are not only important in maintaining secondary levels as an operating program in a viable culture, they are the means by which both may be regularly developed into more satisfying and productive forms. If the interpenetration of school and community can improve the program, it may also have a beneficial effect on learning and growth among members of families and the community. If a reciprocal process of development could occur, the highest potential of education would be in reach.

Methods and materials as well as the learning events involved in secondary levels are described in Chapter 5. If methods are influences organized to increase the likelihood that the desired learning will occur, then all elements of the support structure should be added to the list of techniques. The support system we create is the method by which we teach. Therefore, specific methods of instruction are embedded in the support structure and draw their long-range effectiveness from it. In light of these influences, Coleman's conclusion that changes in method alone do not significantly change even achievement on tests is understandable. When system and program are congruent in the learning situation, the influence of method as support structure is increased and more beneficial effects on learning may be achieved.

Support Principle 9: Many innovations have been recommended in recent years, many attempts at implementation have been conducted, and many adoptions have been announced. But the programs of the mass of secondary schools have changed little. There is no apparent structure or strategy for accomplishing major changes presently operating which can be employed to implement new programs or settings such as secondary levels and its support system.

When programs have an appropriate support structure, their chances of functioning successfully are considerably increased. Unless the process includes promising strategies for implementing the program and structure, however, that proposition may never be tested.

The recent record of school change is not good. In *Behind the Classroom Door* John Goodlad concludes from his study of innovations:

> Many of the changes we have believed to be taking place in schooling have not been getting into classrooms; changes widely recommended for the schools over the past 15 years were blunted on school and classroom doors. Second, schools and classrooms were marked by a sameness regardless of location, student enrollment, and typing as provided initially to us by an administrator.

Summarizing a number of studies of school changes, John Pincus states:

> The responses of schools to opportunities for innovation appear therefore to be complex; and between the adoption and the implementation, innovations routinely disappear or suffer sea changes.

In the absence of competitive marketplace conditions, the choice of innovations by a school or district is influenced by bureaucratic safety, response to external pressure, and approval among bureaucratic peer elites. Thus administrators are reluctant to collaborate with other social groups to make policy and are unlikely to implement any but the most marginal changes. Those which are adopted, Pincus says, tend to promote the image of the school as up-to-date, efficient, professional, and responsive to the community, rather than to change the learning experience of children.

Many other explanations have been written about the failure of innovation and the durability of familiar schooling, attributing it to: the adequacy of present programs, natural individual resistance to change, the erosion of new practices into familiar ones, lack of marketplace conditions among schools, the failure of innovators to deal with the well-established complexities of school culture, lack of clear and demonstrably superior alternatives, and failure of schools to develop a built-in system of renewal. Others may attribute it to the conservatism of teachers, the demands of parents, the intransigence of administrators, and the self-serving tendencies of academics. And many alternatives have been recommended: increasing funds for innovations, adapting changes to the target school, using methods of humanizing or otherwise changing school personnel, decentralizing the district school system, permitting students to choose among alternative schools, lowering the age of compulsory education, using different methods of planning, including a greater range of representation in planning, and training teachers as change agents. Despite these explanations and recommendations, apparently no operating procedure can be employed to implement a planned change or to stimulate a school to plan major improvements when the decision to do so is not its own. For this reason, Harvey Averch and his associates advise that the only way to institute school change is compulsion—some outside force must deliver shocks so powerful the traditional system must respond to survive.

Each of the separate recommendations for managing the changeover process seems promising but limited. Funds can often stimulate new practices within the limited range of acceptability to the school system. Lighthouse schools may demonstrate lighthouse practice, but they have little influence on other schools and are often extinguished when funding ends. Adapting innovations to the target population to reduce resistance may increase the odds in favor of their adoption but may also reduce the significance of the innovation by minimizing the degree of change involved and by avoiding the problem of support structure and school culture which tend to maintain programs. Changing schools by administering shocks to the bureaucracy such as the implementation of a voucher system does promise variety in schools and increases the opportunity for teachers to work and students to study with like-minded colleagues, but the apparent assumption that members of the bureaucracy know what should be done and how to do it, and will under irresistible pressure, may be false on all counts. Although local school planning will insure diversity in the alternative schools, it seems possible that such schools may offer only one form of learning experience to students, and each may develop its own rigid bureaucracy, closed system of operation, and increased isolation. No matter how promising, most strategies for implementing change seem to deal with only part of the problem: They are designed to implement a portion of the program or to modify one dimension of the system.

In addition, change in the educational setting is often conducted as an imposition in which a change in program, determined by an outside agency, is introduced to the setting with or without the approval of the participants. Change may also be conducted organically by increasing the opportunity and ability of participants to determine how it shall be improved. While both involve intervention, they are different in kind and purpose. The first is an attempt to manipulate the program, often in spite of the culture of the setting; the second is an attempt to create a setting in which the participants are better able to manipulate the program themselves.* While the imposed innovation may be logically sound, manipulation to impose is not, because it both arouses resistance and does little to cultivate the personal growth or relationships of participants, whose influence on learning is likely much greater than any instrument of teaching they may employ. The more promising approach is one in which the setting is improved by providing opportunities, guarantees, resources, and consultation for participants to develop better programs themselves, and in the process to develop relationships which cultivate rather than hinder their personal and professional renewal.

Support Principle 10: Major development in secondary education may be accomplished as a clearly specified shift in program combined with a strategy for comprehensive change in the setting in which it occurs. A comprehensive strategy for implementing secondary levels may include educational governance by a large, broadly representative assembly; a constitution assuring the rights and responsibilities of all participants; a process of program development review; a regional committee of educational agencies and business organizations for cooperative programming; diversified teaching centers; a sustained staff development process with the assistance of specialists; and the use of many aides and experts in the community.

This proposed approach to significantly increasing the beneficial effects of secondary education on student learning involves three related propositions: 1) that major change in the program can best be accomplished in a coherent reconstruction of all learning events; 2) that a shift in the program requires a shift in structure adapting all aspects of the management system to provide the best setting to cultivate the program's operation; and 3) that the program is best implemented through a comprehensive strategy in this appropriate setting. An attempt has been made in this

*For a thorough explanation of this process, see Sarason (1971, 1972) and Goodlad (1972, 1975).

chapter to outline the basic elements of the support structure and how they can be adapted to secondary levels. If these do form the necessary setting, an attempt must now be made to describe a comprehensive strategy for implementing them.

Individually Guided Education, (IGE) now employed in hundreds of American elementary schools, is described by Herbert J. Klausmeier as a "comprehensive alternative system of schooling designed to produce higher educational achievements by providing effectively for differences among students. . . ." The elements of this comprehensive system include the multi-unit school organization, an individual instructional programming process, a procedure for evaluating student learning, the development of compatible curriculum materials, a program of home-school-community relations, establishment of a supportive environment, and commitments to continuing research and development and to implementation through a four-phase procedure. This new program, apparently successful in achieving wide acceptance in individual schools, first suggested that a comprehensive strategy for change was essential. An operational model, IGE should be examined as an alternative to the untested comprehensive strategy for implementing secondary levels. One other successful model of implementation, the one by which our present system of schooling was established, was also comprehensive.

A comprehensive strategy is ecological because elements necessary to support the new program are established and integrated into a coherent setting which promotes its adoption and growth. Strategies for implementing these diverse elements include:

1. A conference to establish an education assembly. Martin and Harrison recommend that a respected group—not associated with education, politics, or a lobby position—call a communitywide conference to establish a large, representative district education assembly made up of representatives from education and from the community.

2. Determination by the assembly of an over-all plan for district educational services and the appointment of program and management committees, including the secondary levels advisory council.

In such decisions the assembly would require the assistance of a representative of the state government to explain the legal requirements they are bound to meet, representatives from universities and other institutions ι discuss alternatives, and representatives of other districts to share solutions to planning problems. In keeping with the concept of lifelong learning, the purpose of the plan would be to provide suitable and powerful educational experiences for all ages and sectors in the community and to integrate them in the educational life of the community. Secondary levels is most appropriately conceived as part of such a network.

3. A commission appointed by the assembly to draft the district educational constitution. The draft, once approved in the assembly, would then be circulated throughout the district for discussion, and finally presented for ratification in a district by-election. Wide discussion is particularly important because assigned roles, rights, responsibilities, and authority, and confirmed procedures for planning, deciding, implementing, managing, and developing as set down in the constitution would affect all participants—educators and members of the community.

4. Implementation of an open, rational process for planning, approval, implementation, and review of programs in the various centers.

This is the central process of program development guaranteed by the constitution and employed throughout the district. Guides to this process include Ralph Tyler's four-step procedure; Hilda Taba's teaching-learning unit based on diagnosis, evaluation, and modification; Ronald Havelock's decision-making procedure based on relationships, diagnosis, and resources; and recommendations for the development of institutions such as Seymour Sarason's suggestion of participation by all groups affected by decisions and consideration of the universe of alternatives before decisions are made.

5. The establishment of working relationships among various sectors of the community involved in education through extensive consultation and the appointment of a high-level committee.

The commitment of organizations in the community to share their personnel and resources for educational purposes depends upon direction from the highest levels of authority and their willingness to cooperate with the assembly and with each other to provide quality services.

6. The establishment of conditions which cultivate and enable the educational operations of the district by the state government, the courts, and the assembly.

The state government could review its laws and provide extra funding for a five-year period of development for districts introducing governance of educational services for all citizens under an assembly, and could consider legislating such services when it was proved that they are possible, fiscally feasible, and educationally desirable. The courts could ratify these rights or insist upon them. In *Robinson* v. *Cahill* the New Jersey Supreme Court ruled that "a thorough and efficient" education, required by the state, be defined so that a finance system could be implemented assuring each child the opportunity to receive that kind of education. The assembly can contribute by judiciously monitoring the decision-making system, fulfilling its obligations to support the implementation of decisions made according to the district constitution, and by granting the rewards of the system to those who develop exemplary services.

7. The creation of a distinctive physical setting for each of the diverse centers in secondary levels by selecting an environment suitable for its function.

In a system of schools comprising very similar buildings and both interior and exterior environments, the concept of diverse physical settings adapted to diverse programs will be unfamiliar. Preplanning by center staffs will enable them to argue for the kind of setting the program requires, to negotiate for an available location, and to initiate long-range planning for the creation of one specially designed for their operations as the program matures. To assist in planning a center for multiple use and with community participation, consulting architects may be engaged, and a step-by-step pattern language for design by groups may be used.

8. The creation of a cooperative cultural setting in each center by assuring the autonomy of each staff and by increasing interaction among staffs.

Guaranteeing the autonomy of each staff to develop its own program, yet holding it responsible to defend the program's worth and to pursue its improvement, may draw participants together to meet the common challenge. The size of each center can be smaller than the average high school, permitting more personal relationships, yet be well equipped because all students will eventually utilize its facilities. Other advantages of diverse centers, summarized by Vernon Smith, include better conditions for community participation, for adaptation of the program to students, and for continuous development of the program, the organization, and the facilities—all of which can improve the culture of the school.

While the schools are diverse, the staffs of each will have many common problems and will benefit from informal meetings to share ideas, perhaps in the league model described by John Goodlad and reported since as a successful model of school change, improving the culture of the school by encouraging supportive relationships among teachers. A "hub" where teachers in the district can meet informally and a consultative relationship between staffs in the league and a team of university specialists are also features of this model. Regular meetings among members of the same kind of center from different districts, perhaps in regional conferences, could have a similar effect on the professional socialization of staff in secondary levels.

    9. The development of alternative teacher training programs at colleges of education.

Secondary levels teachers will require new skills and must be prepared for different tasks in each center. Teacher education programs will be required to develop alternative programs of choice. Because the teaching skills and programs will be developed first in secondary levels schools, teacher education will benefit from close association with secondary levels centers and by emphasizing supervised on-site practice. This would facilitate consultation between professors and staffs and would stimulate new areas of research to solve problems and verify advantages certain to arise in the new system. Teacher education, consultation, and research conducted by a professional team in cooperation with a league of secondary levels schools could be mutually beneficial and contribute significantly to a successful shift. Training lay personnel would become a major task of the district and teacher training institutions.

    10. Production of teaching materials uniquely adapted to the new programs.

Teachers are assisted in their tasks and are more willing to pursue new kinds of instructional tasks when suitable teaching materials are available. If the implementation of secondary levels began on a scale sufficiently large to interest the education industry, software and equipment would soon be researched and developed.

    These ten elements outline one possible comprehensive strategy for the implementation of a management system through which education can be converted to the new form. Ironically, a district may adopt and use the decision-making process designed for implementing and operating secondary levels but choose a different program. The degree to which the structure is established, however, will determine the degree of conversion to the new model. By shaping the medium, we shape the nature of the lesson we wish to teach; by enabling participants to design the lesson itself, we balance measured uncertainty with the greater possibility that it will be adapted to them and regularly improved.

Many of the individual strategies—the league model, diverse centers, the decision-making process, and so on—can be instituted independently. But without a comprehensive plan for an as yet undefined minimum necessary change in program and structure, the change achieved will be limited. Edward Hall says:

> The relationship between man and the cultural dimension is one in which both *man and his environment participate in molding each other.* Man is now in a position of creating the total world in which he lives. . . . In creating this world he is actually determining *what kind of organism* he will be.

Education, as a major element of the environment, plays a major role in determining what its individuals will become. The education environment includes a program and a setting. When both are changed to have a new, coherent effect on students—as well as the other participants—the impact could be powerful. Faced with such a possibility, we must be certain of our aspirations about what kind of organism we wish our youth to become.

Conclusion

The propositions, program elements, and support principles which comprise the Platform Statement of this Task Force outline a major transformation in secondary education, one with implications for learning at every stage of life. A much more temperate, generalized statement, one more readily supported with evidence, more demonstrably workable, more assured of winning acceptance than stimulating debate, could have been written. But it now seems more important to consider a transformation of consciousness about education and of the process as a whole than additional modifications of instructional materials and teaching methods and further demands for research. It is time to join these separate efforts into a single force determined to create a form of education with evident benefits for the transformation and transition of youth—and, as a result—for the community as well.

The second wave of settlers—perhaps the first as well—came to this continent with the hope of developing a new life and a new world in a strange, threatening wilderness. And they did. Now, standing in the strange, threatening wilderness that world has become, we must find a new vision, a new process, a new continent of hope in this same land—and we must journey toward it with confidence in our ability to deal with whatever difficulties confront us. This Platform Statement aspires to that urgent purpose.

APPENDIX I
DISSENTING OPINIONS

B. Frank Brown
Director, Information and Services
Institute for Development of Educational
Activities, Inc.

Chapter 1

If I correctly understand the sentence which calls for the abolition of hierarchial distinctions among students, primary teachers, and university professors, then I dissent. Authority is an important value in a democracy and the school should be the last place to propose that it be vitiated.

The Task Force was charged with the task of determining "whether or not it would be advantageous to lower the age of compulsory education; and if it did, to determine for what reasons and by what means it should be done, and what alternatives should be made available to students." Unfortunately, we did not have the courage to deal with the issue. Instead, we broadened the scope of our charge to include transition for youth and made this the major concentration of our effort.

The issue of compulsory attendance in schooling is volatile and those who advocate it are destined to be rebuked with more than their share of polemics. But this is no excuse for pusillanimity in dealing with the issue.

The argument to eliminate compulsory schooling is based upon the urgent need to abolish the custodial responsibility of the high schools. Three factors make custodianship impossible to administer: 1) the earlier maturation of youth; 2) numerous legal and quasi-legal rights extended to young people of school age—especially the Supreme Court's conferring of First Amendment rights on school children in the *Tinker* case; and 3) the lessening in the concept of authority as a value for youth.

Another factor which makes forced schooling impractical is the mushrooming number of assaults and other crimes in the schools. This has reached an unbelievable statistic. The chairman of the Senate Committee on the Judiciary, after a year-long investigation of juvenile delinquency, reported recently, "The number of students who died in the combat zones of the nation's schools between 1970 and 1973 exceeds the number of American soldiers killed in the first three years of the Vietnam conflict." The cost of vandalism now exceeds the cost of the nation's textbooks.

I cannot accept the point of view in the report of the bleeding-heart liberals who contend that lowering the school-leaving age will mean that all of the disadvantaged children will drop out of school. There is no evidence to support this reasoning but, on the other hand, considerable evidence to support the notion that poor and disadvantaged people now have more faith in schools than average, middle-class people.

But the most forceful argument for lowering the compulsory attendance age is the fact that the law is not enforced. Average daily attendance is dropping in all states and is at 48 percent in the inner-city schools of New York City. Students everywhere are flouting the compulsory attendance laws with full knowledge that nothing will happen to them. I submit that this is the wrong kind of climate in which to rear young people. If youth are to be brought up to understand citizenship and respect the law, then legislation relating to compulsory school attendance must be either rigidly enforced or abolished. The issue of compulsory attendance needs to be dealt with forcefully and responsibly. As a Task Force, we skirted the issue.

Chapter 2

I dissent from the statement, "The Task Force seeks a definition which emphasizes the development and maturity of students rather than their mastery of subjects. . . ." This is unrealistic, indefensible, and flies in the face of what is actually happening in education—a return to the basics. The mastery of subject matter must remain a central focus of schools; and certainly one of the chief purposes of schooling is to support and sustain a literate society.

Chapter 6

I dissent from the general notion that the schools should become deeply involved in all kinds of alternatives for students. Agreed, there should be an increasing number of alternatives for youth, but the alternatives must be community based. Therefore, if the alternative program is to be successful, it should be administered by a community board outside the school. Teachers and principals have neither the training, experience, nor expertise to organize and operate community-based alternatives to conventional schooling. If meaningful alternatives are established, then they must be directed by service-minded adults in the community.

Francis X. Sutman, Chairman
Department of Secondary Education, Temple University

My statement must not be considered simply as dissent; rather it is an opinion growing out of learning through involvement in the Task Force debates and through reading and editing of the manuscript. Dissent implies closure. But is not this report of the Task Force debates committed to lifelong open or continuing education? That's what it is all about!

It is true, as indicated in Frank Brown's dissenting comments, that the Task Force was originally brought together to consider the issue of lowering the compulsory age of education as recommended in several commission reports, including *The Reform of Secondary Education.* However, some members of the PDK Task Force rapidly endorsed the concept of opportunity for lifelong education. Any statement regarding an age at which youngsters could legally drop out of school is incompatible with the above position. Unfortunately, however, it does not quite eliminate discussion concerning a possible legal dropout age of 14 years.

In my opinion, our education system of the future should eliminate any possibility for dropping out. Instead, "schooling" should become woven so deeply into the fabric of community life that option after option is available to everyone. It should be clear, however, that I do continue to support the idea that there is a basic education in skills essential to every mentally capable person preparing to contribute to the well-being of society. Reducing the compulsory age is in disagreement with this objective, while lifelong education as developed in Chapter 5 of this PDK Task Force Report is not!

Continued debate on the issues presented in the report, as suggested, is important. Communication and interaction must continue; however, now is a time also for action! Too few emerging adults are being adequately served by the traditional secondary school. And every year millions more emerge into adulthood ill-equipped for their role and even less equipped to continue the learning process.

A report of the fall, 1975 Conference of the New Jersey Council of School Administration states that schools can "change rapidly; they are a flexible institution." Experience does not show this to be true. Secondary schools are particularly rigid. Only action programs will overcome this rigidity. I refer the reader to a proposal for action that I presented in the summer, 1974 issue of the *Journal of Teacher Education* in the article, "Let's Start the Future Today!"

Finally, this PDK Task Force Report briefly mentions needed changes in teacher education programs. I would have liked to have seen more emphasis on this aspect of education, for without flexible, quality teachers, all is lost. Today's society does not set high priority on quality teacher education, much less on the education of teachers to deal with lifelong education. I would propose that PDK or AACTE organize a new task force to deal with recommendations for quality teacher education designed to prepare personnel who will be able to function effectively in the school setting described in the PDK Task Force Report.

Scott D. Thomson
Associate Secretary for Research, NASSP

We should not play Hamlet with compulsory education. Society must assume responsibility for youth, for their education and their transition, and society should not waffle on this responsibility.

What are required today are broader definitions of education and specific arrangements for implementing these broader definitions. Learning ought to extend beyond the classroom. Youth may be educated in a variety of locales. But in each instance, objectives need clearly to be stated and avenues for program delivery identified.

Society should develop a variety of arrangements for students to learn and to develop until youth have either earned the high school diploma or reached the age of legal majority. At either of these points in life the student will assume adult status and move beyond those conditions fairly required by society to prepare youth for this adult status.

American society has not assumed sufficient responsibility in the past for the education and transition of youth. Requiring compulsory attendance at school to age 16 is only a faint attempt to meet responsibilities. Requiring compulsory school attendance to age 14 would simply weaken an already limited overall effort. What now makes sense is a program of education for youth, broadly conceived, using the resources of the entire community under the management of the school. The expectation is that by careful planning and imaginative deployment all youth may be served—some on campus, some off campus, and the balance by various mixes of environment. Youth would move toward adulthood in a purposeful manner according to a variety of needs and conditions.

The arrangements cannot be helter-skelter. They may not be laissez faire. Rather, while the opportunities for

growth and learning would be enlarged, the design should
be specific. Plans would be laid out, objectives and expectations defined, and supervision and evaluation planned.

All youth possess the potential to grow intellectually
and socially when adequately assisted. The conditions
for this growth must be provided within a context broader
than traditionally has been available to youth. But this
position is a substantially different one from proposing a
situation of schooling or work at age 14 or of creating
new agencies to care for "nonschool" youth at age 14.

The central problem of compulsory education histori-
cally has been one of limited definition, of a dwarfish application of the vision. The vision itself meets contemporary
conditions. Youth should be transformed for adulthood
under a cohesive and flexible program of education arranged by society. Youth cannot fend for themselves in a
complex society. They should not be cut adrift.

APPENDIX II
MODEL PROGRAMS

Schools and Programs Where Elements of the Platform Statement Are Already in Action

This catalog intends to acquaint the reader with a cross section of schools and programs containing elements of the PDK Task Force Platform Statement.

1. Action-Learning Program
   Ames High School, Ames, Iowa

   Most students at some time during their high school experiences spend a part of their time doing volunteer work in the community. Volunteer service includes tutoring of younger children and work in hospitals, churches, public institutions, day-care centers, and retirement homes.

   This is one of many "action-learning" models presently in operation. Further information about this type of school can be obtained by reading "Some Action-Learning Models," by Diane Hedin and Dan Conrad, in the *NASSP Bulletin*, November, 1974, pp. 22-28. The booklet *25 Action-Learning Schools* published by the National Association of Secondary School Principals also outlines the "action-learning" concept. The description of Ames High School, above, is an abbreviated example of the programs described in this booklet.

2. Applied Education Center
   Beverly Hills High School
   Beverly Hills, California
   Dean Turner, director

   All community-based programs operate from this center. It is, in effect, a new department of the school with its own head. The center identifies and locates community learning stations as well as placing and supervising students. See, also, the Direction Center at

Champaign Valley Community School discussed in
25 *Action-Learning Schools.*

3. Canada World Youth Organization
   Montreal, Quebec

   Three hundred Canadian youths between the ages
of 16 to 20 learn about themselves, others, other cultures, service, and work in a nine-month program. They
spend one month in training; four months working on
service projects in two Canadian communities with a
matching group of students from host foreign countries;
and four months at work in Malaysia, Tunisia, and other
countries. Evaluation of personal growth, the objective
of the program, occurs immediately after the nine-
month experience and two months later in follow-up
sessions.

4. The Central New York External
   High School Diploma Program

   The State Education Department in New York has
financed the demonstration of a new competency-based
high school diploma program for adults. The diploma
recognizes performance in basic skills areas (math,
reading) as well as in life skills (consumer, scientific,
citizenship and health awareness, and occupational
preparedness). It rewards advanced occupational/voca-
tional, academic, and specialized skills. An open testing
technique is characterized by flexibility in time and
location (take-home tests, etc.). One year's successful
employment at the same job with verification by the
employer may be presented as evidence of entry-level
job skills to fulfill the occupational/vocational requirement. Or a performance assessment is arranged on the
job. For a 30-page description of the program, send $2
to the Regional Learning Service, 405 Oak St., Syracuse, NY 13203.

5. City-As-School
   Brooklyn, New York

   A booklet prepared by the board of education of the city of New York describes this program as follows: City-As-School is for juniors or seniors who have completed their math and science requirements (two years each). Students will engage in learning through activity and learning units in agencies, companies, institutions, etc. in all parts of our city, reinforced by tutorial groups and independent study. These units have been planned with the particular organization directly involved.

6. Craig City School
   Craig, Alaska

   This school receives a special grant from the Office of Education—a grant intended to fund comprehensive change in a school over a five-year period. Graduation requirements are based on performance objectives developed by widely representative committees. Minicourses lasting three weeks have been implemented. The school emphasizes practical living skills, academic skills, and career skills for all students. Through close cooperation with the community, many of these skills are taught in the field with the assistance of parents and other adults. Interestingly, staff salaries also are performance based.

7. Quincy Senior High II
   Quincy, Illinois

   This school provides 1500 students in grades 11 and 12 with the opportunity to choose from among seven alternatives within the main school: Traditional School, Flexible School, Project to Individualize Education School, Fine Arts School, Career School, Work-Study School, and Special Education School. A conscious effort is made to match students with the type of school within the school that best suits that student's interests, self-discipline, and learning style.

8. Experience-Based Career Education
   Oakland, California, School District

   The Far West School in Oakland emphasizes learning
through direct experience in adult activities, especially
in employment settings. It merges the traditional academic, general, and vocational tracks in a long-range
attempt to help students select, enter, advance, and find
satisfaction in careers. For information, write Far West
Laboratory, 1855 Folsom St., San Francisco, CA 94102.

9. Individually Guided Education (IGE) Secondary
   Madison, Wisconsin

   The Wisconsin R & D Center for Cognitive Learning
is developing an approach to IGE for secondary schools
to complement the now widespread IGE elementary
program. The secondary project, under the direction of
Patrick Struve, is to design and field-test a number of
processes by which school staffs can plan and develop
their own programs. The common features of these programs are individualized student learning, continuous
progress, and the development of the school as a community resource. A theoretical paper, casebook of operations, and materials for implementation—based upon field
work—were completed in the summer of 1975. A demonstration school is under way, utilizing the planning
procedures. It is available for visits in 1976, if government grants enable the developmental work to continue.

10. Mariner High School
    Mukilteo, Washington
    Cliff Gillies, Principal

    This school has many features suggested in the
Carleton model. For instance, students take the
"critical path" approach to learning, moving at their
own pace. Many community courses are offered, including "Horse Science." All members of the professional
staff act as student advisors, including the principal.
Many senior options exist for credit, similar to some of

the options offered at Carleton. The student can propose and gain approval for a project from such choices as apprenticeships with public officials, travel, social service, archaeological digs, research, or developing a creative talent.

11. The Metro High School
Chicago's School Without Walls

As in other schools without walls, Metro High uses the facilities of the city as classrooms. Students respond especially well to units of study where they feel they can make a unique personal contribution to a group investigation or project.

12. Mini-Walkabout
Campbell River Senior Secondary School
Campbell River, British Columbia

Two teachers and a student teacher started a mini-Walkabout with 46 students over a five-month semester, using a mix of Walkabout challenges, teacher-planned activities called "tasks," and student-planned activities called "projects/challenges." The tasks are tied in with the disciplines of biology, geography, and social studies. For details, write David Brown and Dale Kelley, Environmental Studies Program, Campbell River Senior Secondary School, 350 Dogwood St., Campbell River, B.C., Canada.

13. The Peterborough Project
Peterborough, Ontario

At Thomas A. Stewart Secondary School, in a program funded by the Ontario Department of Education, grades 11 and 12 students spend approximately half the school day working in social agencies in the community. Students have regular work responsibilities and identify one problem of the agency to study and make recommendations for solving it. See Russell, Leithwood, and Baxter, 1973, *The Peterborough Project.*

14. Pilot Walkabout Program
    Ernest W. Seaholm High School
    Birmingham, Michigan

    This program uses the five challenges on the Walk-
about model. Students begin by forming an advisory
committee composed of a teacher-sponsor, their parents,
a community resource person, the principal, and any
student resource person who may be of help. For details,
write John C. Schulz, Principal, Ernest W. Seaholm
High School, 2436 W. Lincoln, Birmingham, MI 48009.

15. Project Advance
    Syracuse University in cooperation with
    Manhassatt High School and 30 others
    Warren McGreagor, Principal

    College courses in such subjects as psychology,
music, English, and government are taught on the high
school campus. Any student may apply and upon satis-
factory completion of the course will receive college
credit.

16. Quest
    Bracebridge and Muskoka Lakes Secondary School
    Bracebridge, Ontario

    Modeled after the program outlined by Maurice
Gibbons in "Walkabout: Searching for the Right Pas-
sage from Childhood and School" (May, 1974, *Phi Delta
Kappan*), Quest features projects to provide five basic
challenges: adventure, creativity, service, practical
skill, and logical inquiry. For details, write K. H. Black,
Principal, Bracebridge and Muskoka Lakes Secondary
School, Bracebridge, Ontario, Canada.

17. The REAL Program
    North Bethesda Junior High School
    Bethesda, Maryland

    One of the teachers involved in REAL describes the
program in the following terms: This program involves
125 ninth-grade students. The focal concern is to pre-

pare students to be responsible citizens. Students register every six weeks for their four major REAL courses.
Students plan a schedule and then sign up with each
teacher. During nonclass time students do a variety of
things, including community work. Recently included in
the program is a formal grievance procedure for airing
teacher and student complaints and reaching decision
by all concerning the merits of each case.

18. Resource Center for Environmental Education
    New York, New York

    In this program, students leave their schools one day
    each week to attend environmental workshops in the
    Federal Hall National Monument in New York City.
    (This program and many others will be described in
    a 1976 NSSE Yearbook chapter being prepared by
    Vernon H. Smith and Robert D. Barr.)

19. St. Paul Open School
    St. Paul, Minnesota

    A bulletin describing the St. Paul Open School gives
    the following description of how it works: "With the
    help of their advisors and parents, students plan their own
    programs. These programs develop from the students'
    own goals, interests, learning styles, and strengths.
    Students may choose from among classes on a trimester
    schedule, their own independent study in the building
    or at a community agency or business, or participate
    in open lab activities. Progress toward goals is discussed
    regularly with advisors and at least four times a year
    with parents." For further information, contact St. Paul
    Open School, 1885 University Ave., St. Paul, MN 55104.

20. School and Community Service Project
    Rampo, New York

    In this project, many community services are being
    provided by students, including:
    1. Mental Health Complex in Pomona: students play

games with patients, organize activities, and read and tell stories.

2. New York Rehabilitation Hospital in Haverstraw: students help with physical therapy.

3. West Street Day Care Center in Spring Valley: students work with children ages 3 to 5.

4. Rockland County Infirmary in Pomona: students write letters for patients, take them for walks, and lead discussion groups.

5. Camp Jawonio in New York: students assist in developing physical skills in the physically handicapped through therapy and games.

6. Boy Scouts in New City: students help organize new troops and assist with their camping programs. (For details, see National Commission on Resources for Youth, ibid.)

21. The Senior Year: A Laboratory for Living
Wissahickon School District
Ambler, Pennsylvania

This project emphasizes long-term social involvement, volunteer effort, involvement with older and younger people, productive work, and opportunity to "try oneself" in real life, classroom discussion, and sharing of field experiences. For details, write Albert B. Jacobs, Director of Secondary Education, Wissahickon School District, Ambler, PA 19002.

22. State of Oregon
The June 9, 1975 edition of the *Saturday Review* included this description of the State of Oregon education policy: Students cannot get their high school diplomas until they have demonstrated competence in the everyday, practical skills necessary for getting and holding a job, managing a household, and participating in the political and social life of the community. By 1970 the Oregon State Board of Education had identified 10 broad areas of competency required for "personal development, social responsibility, and career develop-

ment." The individual school districts were asked to subdivide these basic competencies into as many as 35 to 250 specific real-life skills and to devise standards for measuring student proficiency in each.

23. The Walkabout Project in North Central High School
    Indianapolis, Indiana
    Gary Phillips, coordinator

With the help of a $970,000 grant from the Lilly Foundation, the North Central High School began a Walkabout project in the fall of 1974. The major thrust is to model a number of innovations for the 200-plus regular teachers at North Central High and in the feeder junior highs, so it is a major inservice program. The curriculum is built around seven challenge areas: volunteer service, cognitive skills, practical skills, creativity, futurism and decision making, research and inquiry, and adventure. Students create a project in each of these areas each semester. Community resources are heavily used, parents are greatly involved, and the curricula are totally individualized. Parents, students, and teachers write their own curricula. Among special features: a large computer-assisted instruction component.

APPENDIX III

Roles and Responsibilities of Participants
in the Secondary Level Learning Life-Style Model

A brief description of the roles implicit in the Learning Life-Style model are:

a. Student Role: As an individual, to learn to develop his or her own abilities; as a participant in the educating process, to learn to design his or her own learning activities and to contribute to the learning activities of others; as a member of society, to learn to take part in the work, recreation, service, and functioning of the community.

b. Parent's Role: As a parent, to encourage the child's development by representing self-directed learning and participation in the educating process and in the life of the community; as a participant in the educating process, to cooperate with the child in developing his or her own learning and with other adults in the planning and implementation of the educational program in such specific roles as:

   1. Aide: assisting the teacher or other adults instructing.
   2. Tutor: assisting a single student in the skills program or in the accomplishment of some task.
   3. Master: teaching something for which he or she is highly qualified in the differentiated schools.
   4. Manager: supervising the collection and distribution of placements in the community.

   As a member of the society, to model, and therefore to teach, responsible participation in, and use of, the community.

c. Other Community Members: As members of the community-at-large, to participate in the educating process by teaching students the skills of their vocations, providing real on-the-job experience and offering them a relationship of mutual respect; and as members of the service, business, and professional sectors of the community, to conduct their affairs in a way which models responsible as well as skilled behavior.

d. Teacher's Role: As a person, to represent a life of active personal and professional development; as a participant in the educating process, to guide and provide group leadership in the students' design of their own learning and to manage learning systems as well as provide direct instruction; and as a member of society, to cooperate with adults in designing educational programs in the community.

e. School Board and Department of Education Officials: As participants in the educating process, to assist in planning and implementing new programs; as official representatives of the community, to manage the supporting services for the program, to negotiate necessary new policies with union officials, lawyers, businessmen, universities, and so on, and to manage the budget.

f. Experts: Specialists such as professors, researchers, clinical psychologists, reading experts, doctors, and so on, to act as consultants providing data, resources, and skill necessary for program decisions and implementation by the advisory council and its constituency.

Statement f underlines the shift, recommended here, from programs designed by experts with possible student, teacher, and citizen consultation to programs designed by students, teachers, and other adults with necessary consultation of experts. This means that the process precedes the program. While the program model presented earlier is recommended, the process of community decision making may modify it considerably.

Each of these role descriptions involves a major shift in responsibilities compared to general practice as it presently exists:

a. student   required courses designed by others, but little responsibility for general program of his or her own once choices made.   required accomplishment within frameworks for designing one's own learning (differentiated schools, skill program, challenge tasks).

Learning becomes the student's work.

b. parent   supplies the taxes and the student, but generally an outsider to educational process.   shares responsibility for planning educational program, may work in it, consults with child and school on choice of learning tasks.

Responsibility for the educating process is shared by the parent working with the school and the child.

c. other community members   possibly involved in school board by vote or participation and taxes.   involved in planning the educational program, may work in it providing direct experience and training for student in the community.

Every adult shares responsibility for participation in youth's preparation for life and work in the community.

d. teacher   teaches assigned courses and assigned content.   plans programs with other adults in the community; guides and teaches students so that they can perform on their own.

Teachers share the educating process with community members, guide learning, and become continuing students of the what and how of education.

e. school officials   dictate the nature of the program, organization, and facilities; set rules and conditions of administration, teaching, and learning.   participate in planning and manage the creation of organizations, facilities, and regulations to make the new programs possible.

School officials become experts in creating and managing the organization necessary for the implementation of new programs rather than authorities who maintain familiar programs by maintaining traditional patterns of organization.

f. experts   design programs directly by involvement in curriculum planning or indirectly through publications.   consult in planning process or resource to officials, teachers, parents, and students.

Experts become responsible consultants in program planning rather than directors and are obliged to convince others as equals.

APPENDIX IV

CHALLENGE PROPOSAL

Sponsor: _____ Name _____

Community Sponsor: _____

Category of Challenge: _____

1. State your proposal as a challenge. Be specific. State the kind of performance and the level of performance you will pursue.

2. Outline the preparation you will need: training, practice, information gathering, and so on.

3. List the resources you will require. (equipment, people, work space, transportation, materials, money)

4. What is the greatest obstacle you expect to encounter?

5. What positive sources can you draw on to overcome this obstacle?

6. What is your first step in launching this Walkabout?

7. List the other steps that lead to the completion of your challenge:

8. What form will your presentation or demonstration of accomplishment take?

9. Proposed date of completion:

10. Signature of Approval

Parent: _____

Sponsor: _____

Community Sponsor: _____

BIBLIOGRAPHY

Alexander, Christopher; Ishikawa, Sara; and Silverstein, Murray. *A Pattern Language Which Generates Multiservice Centers*. Berkeley, Calif.: Center for Environmental Structure, 1968.

Alexander, Kern and Jordan, K. Forbis. *Legal Aspects of Educational Choice; Compulsory Attendance and Student Assignment*. Topeka, Kan.: National Organization on Legal Problems in Education, 1973.

Arons, Stephen *et al. Doing Your Own School: A Practical Guide to Starting and Operating a Community School*. Boston: Beacon Press, 1972.

_____ . "The Separation of School and State: Pierce Reconsidered." Unpublished draft, January, 1976.

Averch, Harvey A.; Carroll, Stephen J.; Donaldson, Theodore S.; Kiesling, Herbert J.; and Pincus, John. *How Effective Is Schooling? A Critical Review of Research*. Englewood Cliffs, N.J.: Educational Technology Publications, 1974.

Bayh, Birch. *Our Nation's Schools—A Report Card: "A" in School Violence and Vandalism* (Preliminary Report of the U.S. Senate Subcommittee to Investigate Juvenile Delinquency). Washington, D.C.: U.S. Government Printing Office, 1975.

Bellanca, James and Kirschenbaum, Howard. *College Guide for Experimenting High Schools*. Upper Jay, N.Y.: Adirondack Mountain Humanistic Education Center, 1973.

Bennis, Warren G.; Benne, Kenneth D.; and Chin, Robert. *The Planning of Change*. 2nd ed. New York: Holt, Rinehart and Winston, 1969.

Bereiter, Carl. *Must We Educate?* Englewood Cliffs, N.J.: Prentice-Hall, 1973.

Berg, Ivan. *Education and Jobs: The Great Training Robbery*. New York: Praeger, 1970.

Borowsky, George *et al. Yellow Pages of Learning Resources*. Cambridge, Mass.: The MIT Press, 1972.

Braybrooke, David and Lindbolom, Charles E. *A Strategy of Decision*. New York: The Free Press, 1963.

Bremer, John and von Moschzisker, Michael. *The School Without Walls: Philadelphia's Parkway Program*. New York: Holt, Rinehart and Winston, 1971.

Brown, B. Frank. *The Appropriate Placement School*. W. Nyack, N.Y.: Parker, 1965.

_____. *The Nongraded High School*. W. Nyack, N.Y.: Parker, 1965.

_____ *et al. The Reform of Secondary Education*. New York: McGraw-Hill, 1973.

Brown, Barbara B. *New Mind, New Body; Bio-Feedback: New Directions for the Mind*. New York: Harper and Row, 1974.

Brown, George Isaac. *Human Teaching for Human Learning: An Introduction to Confluent Education*. New York: Viking, 1971.

Cawelti, Gordon. *Vitalizing the High School: A Curriculum Critique of Major Reform Proposals.* Washington, D.C.: Association for Supervision and Curriculum Development, 1974.

Coleman, James S. *The Adolescent Society.* New York: Free Press, 1961.

_____. *Policy Research in the Social Sciences.* Morristown, N.J.: General Learning Press, 1972.

_____. *et al. Equality of Educational Opportunity.* Washington, D.C.: U.S. Government Printing Office, 1966.

_____ *et al. Youth: Transition to Adulthood* (Report of the Panel on Youth of the President's Science Advisory Committee). Chicago: The University of Chicago Press, 1974.

Conant, James B. *The American High School Today.* New York: McGraw-Hill, 1959.

Conference Report on American Youth in the Mid-Seventies. Washington, D.C.: National Association of Secondary School Principals, 1972.

Cremin, Lawrence. *The Transformation of the School.* New York: Vintage, 1961.

DeBono, Edward. *New Think: The Use of Lateral Thinking in the Generation of New Ideas.* New York: Basic Books, 1968.

Developing New Models, Methods, and Means for Education: A Road Department Look at Public Schooling (/I/D/E/A/ Special Report). Dayton: Institute for Development of Educational Activities, 1974.

Erickson, Donald A., ed. *Public Controls for Nonpublic Schools.* Chicago: University of Chicago Press, 1969.

Erickson, Erik H. *Childhood and Society.* New York: Norton, 1964.

_____. *Identity, Youth, and Crisis.* New York: Norton, 1968.

Fantini, Mario D. *Public Schools of Choice: A Plan for the Reform of American Education.* New York: Simon and Schuster, 1973.

_____. *What's Best for the Children? Resolving the Power Struggle Between Parents and Teachers.* New York: Doubleday, 1974.

Faure, Edgar *et al. Learning To Be; The World of Education Today and Tomorrow.* Paris: Unesco, 1972.

Flavell, John H. *The Developmental Psychology of Jean Piaget.* Princeton, N.J.: Van Nostrand, 1963.

Friedenberg, Edgar Z. *Coming of Age in America: Growth and Acquiescence.* New York: Random House, 1965.

Gagne, Robert M. *The Conditions of Learning.* New York: Holt, Rinehart and Winston, 1965.

Gibbons, Maurice. *Individualized Instruction: An Analysis of the Programs.* New York: Teachers College Press, 1972.

_____. "The Search for a Powerful Method of Training Teachers." In *The Teacher's Changing Role in the School of the Future.* Beirut: World Confederation of Organizations of the Teaching Profession, 1972.

——————. "Walkabout: Searching for the Right Passage from Childhood and School." *Phi Delta Kappan*, May, 1974, pp. 596-602.

Glasser, Barney G. and Strauss, Anselm L. *Status Passage: A Formal Theory*. Chicago: Aldine Atherton, 1971.

Glasser, William. *Schools Without Failure*. New York: Harper and Row, 1969.

Goodlad, John I.; Klein, M. Francis *et al. Behind the Classroom Door*. Belmont, Calif.: Wadsworth, 1970.

Goodlad, John I. "The Child and His School in Transition." *The National Elementary Principal*, January, 1973, pp. 28-34.

——————. *The Dynamics of Educational Change*. New York: McGraw-Hill, 1975.

——————. "Staff Development: The League Model." *Theory into Practice*, October, 1972, pp. 207-14.

Goodman, Paul. *Growing Up Absurd: Problems of Youth in the Organized System*. New York: Random House, 1960.

Gordon, William J. *Synectics: The Development of Creative Capacity*. New York: Collier, 1961.

Guidelines for the Collection, Maintenance, and Dissemination of Pupil Records. Hartford, Conn.: Russell Sage Foundation, 1970.

Hall, Edward T. *The Hidden Dimension*, New York: Anchor, 1966.

Harris, Thomas Anthony. *I'm O.K., You're O.K.* New York: Harper and Row, 1967.

Havelock, Ronald G. *The Change Agent's Guide to Innovation in Education*. Englewood Cliffs, N.J.: Educational Technology Publications, 1973.

Havighurst, Robert James. *Developmental Tasks and Education*. New York: David McKay, 1972.

Hosford, Philip L. *An Instructional Theory: A Beginning*. Englewood Cliffs, N.J.: Prentice-Hall, 1973.

Illich, Ivan. *Deschooling Society*. New York: Harper and Row, 1970.

Jackson, Philip W. *Life in Classrooms*. New York: Holt, Rinehart and Winston, 1968.

Jencks, Christopher *et al. Inequality*. New York: Harper and Row, 1972.

Johnson, Howard M. "Are Compulsory Attendance Laws Outdated?" *Phi Delta Kappan*, December, 1973, pp. 226-32.

Joyce, Bruce and Weil, Marsha. *Models of Teaching*. Englewood Cliffs, N.J.: Prentice-Hall, 1972.

Katz, Michael S. *Class, Bureaucracy, and Schools: The Illusion of Educational Change in America*. New York: Praeger, 1971.

Klausmeier, Herbert J. "IGE: An Alternative Form of Schooling." In *Systems of Individualized Education*, edited by Harriet Talmadge. Berkeley, Calif.: McCutchan, 1975, pp. 48-83.

Kozol, Jonathan. *Free Schools*. Boston: Houghton Mifflin, 1972.

Kubler-Ross, Elisabeth. *On Death and Dying*. New York: Macmillan, 1970.

Kuhn, Thomas S. *The Structure of Scientific Revolutions.* Chicago: The University of Chicago Press, 1962.

Letarte, Clyde E. and Mingey, Jack D. *Community Education: From Program to Process.* Midland, Mich.: Pendell, 1972.

Levin, Malcolm and Simon, Roger I. *The Creation of Educational Settings: A Developmental Perspective.* Toronto: Ontario Institute for Studies in Education, 1973.

"Lifelong Learning: The Back-to-School Boom." *Saturday Review,* September 20, 1975, pp. 14-29.

Litwak, Eugene and Meyer, Henry F. *School, Family, and Neighborhood: The Theory of School Community Relations.* New York: Columbia University Press, 1974.

McClure, Larry and Brian, Carolyn, eds. *Essays on Career Education.* Portland, Ore.: Northwest Regional Educational Laboratory, 1973.

McLuhan, Marshall. *Understanding Media: The Extensions of Man.* New York: McGraw-Hill, 1964.

Marien, Michael. *Alternative Futures for Education: An Annotated Bibliography.* Syracuse, N.Y.: Educational Policy Research Center, 1971.

Martin, John Henry *et al. Report of the National Panel on High Schools and Adolescent Education.* /I/D/E/A/ mimeographed draft, 1974.

_____ and Harrison, Charles H. *Free to Learn: Unlocking and Ungrading American Education.* Englewood Cliffs, N.J.: Prentice-Hall, 1972.

Maslow, Abraham H. *The Farther Reaches of Human Nature.* New York: Viking, 1971.

Matters of Choice: A Ford Foundation Report on Alternative Schools. New York: The Ford Foundation, 1974.

Mayer, Martin. *About Television.* New York: Harper and Row, 1972.

Morrison, Terence and Burton, Anthony, eds. *Options: Reforms and Alternatives for Canadian Education.* Toronto: Holt, Rinehart and Winston, 1973.

National Commission on Resources for Youth. *New Roles for Youth in the School and the Community.* New York: Citation Press, 1974.

Pincus, John. "Incentives for Innovation in the Public Schools." *Review of Educational Research,* vol. 44, pp. 113-143.

Reimer, Everett. *School Is Dead: Alternatives in Education.* Garden City, N.Y.: Doubleday, 1971.

Rickenbacker, William F., ed. *Twelve Years Sentence: Radical Views of Compulsory Schooling.* LaSalle, Ill.: Open Court, 1974.

Rickover, Hyman George. *American Education: A National Failure.* New York: Dutton, 1963.

Riesman, David; Glazer, Nathan; and Denny, Reuel. *The Lonely Crowd: A Study of the Changing American Character.* Garden City, N.Y.: Doubleday, 1953.

Roszak, Theodore, *The Making of a Counter-Culture*. New York: Doubleday, 1969.

Rubens, Edwin P. *Planning for Children and Youth Within National Development Planning*. Geneva: U.N. Research Institute for Social Development and the U.N. Children's Fund, 1967.

Russell, H.; Leithwood, K.; and Baxter, R. *The Peterborough Project: A Case Study of Educational Change and Innovation*. Toronto: Ontario Institute of Studies in Education, 1973.

Sarason, Seymour B. *The Creation of Settings and the Future of Societies*. San Francisco: Jossey-Bass, 1972.

Silberman, Charles E. *Crisis in the Classroom: The Remaking of American Education*. New York: Random House, 1970.

Smith, B. Othanel and Orlosky, Donald. *Socialization and Schooling: The Basics of Reform*. Bloomington, Ind.: Phi Delta Kappa, 1975.

Smith, Vernon H. *Alternative Schools: The Development of Options in Public Education*. Lincoln, Neb.: Professional Educators Publications, 1974.

Stephens, J. M. *The Process of Schooling*. New York: Holt, Rinehart and Winston, 1967.

Stevens, John O. *Awareness: Exploring, Experimenting, Experiencing*. Lafayette, Calif.: Real People Press, 1971.

Sutman, Francis. "Let's Start the Future Today!" *The Journal of Teacher Education*, summer, 1974, pp. 149-150.

Taba, Hilda. *Curriculum Development: Theory and Practice*. New York: Harcourt-Brace, 1962.

Terkel, Studs. *Working*. New York: Random House, 1974.

This We Believe. Secondary School in a Changing Society. Washington, D.C.: National Association of Secondary School Principals, 1975.

Three Issues in Education: Project '76 Leadership Seminars. Bloomington, Ind.: Phi Delta Kappa, 1975.

Toffler, Alvin. *Learning for Tomorrow: The Role of the Future in Education*. New York: Random House, 1974.

Tough, Allen. *The Adult's Learning Projects*. Toronto: Ontario Institute for Studies in Education, 1971.

Twenty-five Action Learning Schools. Reston, Va.: National Association of Secondary School Principals, 1974.

Tyler, Ralph W. *Basic Principles of Curriculum Development*. Chicago: University of Chicago Press, 1950.

Van Matre, Steve. *Acclimatization*. Martinsville, Ind.: American Camping Association, 1972.

Wallace, Robert Keith and Benson, Herbert. "The Physiology of Meditation." *Scientific American*, February, 1972, pp. 85-90.

Weil, Andrews. *The Natural Mind*. Boston: Houghton Mifflin, 1972.

Weinstock, Ruth. *The Greening of the High School*. New York: Educational Facilities Laboratory, 1973.

West, E. G. "The Political Economy of American Public School Legisla-
    tion." *Journal of Law and Economics*, October, 1967, pp. 101-28.
Wilson, Craig L. *The Open Access Curriculum*. Boston: Allyn and Bacon,
    1971.